Creating True Prosperity

WORKBOOK

SHAKTI GAWAIN

NATARAJ

NATARAJ PUBLISHING
A DIVISION OF

NEW WORLD LIBRARY
NOVATO, CALIFORNIA

NATARAJ PUBLISHING
A DIVISION OF

NEW WORLD LIBRARY
14 PAMARON WAY
NOVATO, CA 94949

Editorial: Becky Benenate, Katherine Dieter
Cover Design: Aaron Kenedi
Cover Photograph: Giles Hancock

ISBN 1-57731-036-5
First Printing, June 1998
Printed in Canada on acid-free paper
Distributed by Publishers Group West
10 9 8 7 6 5 4 3 2 1

Contents

Introduction

This is a workbook created to assist you in taking the steps outlined in my book, *Creating True Prosperity*. Some of what was written in that book has been intentionally repeated here to allow the workbook to stand on its own. Most of it is new material focused on engaging you in the process of creating a greater sense of prosperity in your life.

Most people think that being prosperous means having plenty of money. Some may have a fairly clear idea of how much money would make them feel prosperous. "If I earned twice as much as I do now, I would be prosperous," or "If I earned as much as ________ (a specific person he or she knows), I'd be prosperous," or "Prosperity means being a millionaire," or "Winning the lottery would definitely make me prosperous."

Others define prosperity in a less specific way, something along these lines: "Prosperity would be having enough money to do what I want, to have the things I want, and not to feel limited by money concerns. A prosperous person is one who doesn't have to worry about money." In other words, prosperity is a kind of freedom to be, do, and have what you really want without (or with little) restriction or limitation.

Most of us yearn for this kind of liberation from money cares and worries. We have the idea that if only we could somehow earn, inherit, win, beg, borrow, or steal enough money to be prosperous, our financial worries would be over and probably quite a few of our other problems could be solved as well!

The question is, how much is enough money to bring us prosperity? Some people have a specific amount in mind that they feel would do the trick; others just assume that there would be some amount that would work. Yet the sad fact is that most of us do not experience prosperity no matter how much money we earn or have.

It's easy to see why we would not feel prosperous if we make very little money and have to struggle just to survive and get our basic needs met. It's also easy to understand why we don't feel prosperous even if we make a moderate income, but have a lot of financial responsibilities — a family to support, a mortgage to pay, and so on.

Yet many people have the experience of making a considerable amount of money and still not experiencing prosperity. Somehow, when our income increases, our level of financial responsibility seems to rise right along with it. The money seems to go out as fast (or faster) than it comes in, and we find ourselves under more pressure and stress to manage it all. We seem to work longer and harder and find ourselves missing out on many important aspects of life — relaxation, intimacy, spiritual connection, fun.

Oddly enough, many wealthy and successful people, especially as they reach middle age, find themselves yearning for simpler times earlier in their lives, when they had less money, fewer needs, and more time.

So there are things that disrupt and interfere with the experience of prosperity at every level of financial wealth. If you have never been wealthy, it may be difficult to believe or accept that having more money may not automatically make you feel prosperous. Yet you probably know or have met someone who's in this exact predicament — he or she has more money than you and is far from enjoying it. The person is unhappy, uptight, and obviously doesn't feel prosperous.

So, at every level of wealth, from the poorest to the richest, there are problems and pitfalls. Having more money, then, does not necessarily bring fewer problems or greater freedom, nor does it guarantee our security. The truth is, prosperity has less to do with money than most of us think.

So, what is prosperity? *Prosperity is the experience of having plenty of what we truly need and want in life, material and otherwise.*

The key point to understand is that prosperity is an internal experience, not an external state, and it is an experience that is not tied to having a certain amount of money. In fact, while prosperity is in some ways related to money, it is not caused by money. While no amount of financial wealth can guarantee an experience of prosperity, it is possible to experience prosperity at almost any level of income (other than one where our basic physical needs are not being met). Problems exist at every level of income. Prosperity can exist at every level, too.

If we think that money has the power to bring us prosperity, we give away our power to money. When we give our power away to anyone or anything, we ultimately feel controlled by that person or thing. So, in order to not feel controlled (and therefore limited) by how much money we have or don't have, we must keep our sense of power within ourselves.

We fixate on money because we see it as the means to obtaining the things we really want. Often, we forget that it is the means, and it gradually becomes the end. In the pursuit of money, we lose sight of the end we truly desire — an experience of prosperity.

In the modern world, most of us have chosen a lifestyle in which we must deal with money. Money is one aspect of our prosperity, the key to getting what we want in the physical realm. Certainly, without satisfying some of our physical wants and needs, we

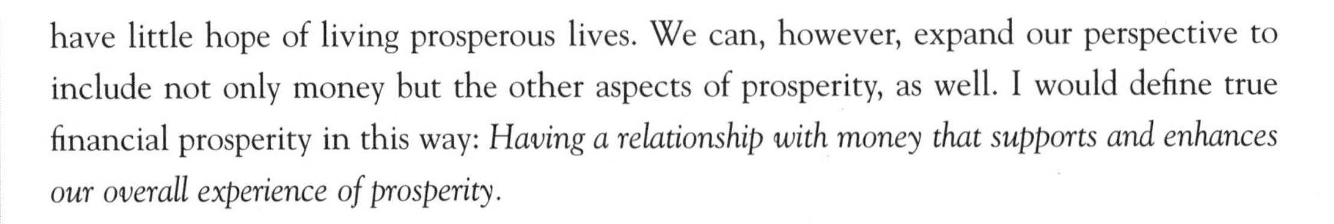

have little hope of living prosperous lives. We can, however, expand our perspective to include not only money but the other aspects of prosperity, as well. I would define true financial prosperity in this way: *Having a relationship with money that supports and enhances our overall experience of prosperity.*

If prosperity is the experience of having plenty of what we truly need and want, then in order to experience it, we must do three things:

1. Find out what we truly need and want.
2. Develop the ability or capacity to bring those things into our lives.
3. Recognize, appreciate, and enjoy what we have.

To whatever degree we can take these three steps, we will experience prosperity at any level of financial wealth that we happen to have.

Every one of us is born into this life with the innate power to make our contribution and to create fulfillment for ourselves. However, this power needs to be developed. Most of us have been wounded during the course of our lives in ways that cause us to doubt or deny our own true power. Feeling somewhat helpless to meet our own needs, we repress them. So most of us go through life fairly unconscious of our own deepest needs and desires.

Deep inside, we feel great yearning, but we don't know exactly what it's for. So we focus on external things, hoping they will bring us satisfaction. Some of them do and some don't, depending on how closely they match what we really want. Ultimately, we don't find lasting satisfaction until we consciously acknowledge our real needs and desires, and learn how to fulfill them.

True prosperity is not something we create overnight. It is not a fixed goal, a place where we finally arrive, or a certain state that we will someday achieve. It is an ongoing process that can continue to unfold and deepen throughout our lives.

To start your process of creating greater prosperity in your life you need to think deeply about what you truly want. What things in life are most important to you?

The things that are most important to me are:

[illegible]
travelling
having good friendships
having money to do what I want and buy what I want.
learning new things
spiritual path
having a nice house

Remember that creating true prosperity does not necessarily mean having more. Many of us are in the predicament of having too much. If we have too many things we don't truly need or want, our lives become overly complicated. This can seriously undermine our experience of prosperity. For many of us, creating true prosperity involves simplifying our lives by clarifying our priorities and letting go of things that we no longer need or that don't bring us real satisfaction.

Also, keep in mind that we do not exist in a vacuum. Our personal experience of prosperity is inextricably linked with our collective prosperity. Using most of the world's natural resources to provide a small percentage of the world's population with material wealth, and leaving the earth depleted and polluted for future generations, is the antithesis of real prosperity. This situation is a reflection of the healing that we need to do individually and collectively.

True prosperity develops as we learn to follow our hearts' true desires and live in balance with ourselves. As we develop this kind of internal integration, we naturally live in greater harmony with others and with the natural world. The greatest personal prosperity can only be experienced in a healthy and prosperous world.

How to Use this Workbook

In *Creating True Prosperity*, I outlined seven steps involved in becoming truly prosperous: Gratitude, Awareness, Healing, Following Your Truth, Creating a Vision, Setting Goals, and Sharing Your Gifts. These steps are not necessarily taken in any particular order. Rather, they describe different elements of the journey. We each have our own unique path. We may focus on each of these elements at various times and in various ways.

At times we may even be working on all of them at once.

The workbook is organized around these seven steps. Feel free to move from one section to another, using the workbook at your own pace. Fill it up, write sideways if you wish, stuff related notes into it. Begin to gather all your feelings, thoughts, and information regarding prosperity in this one special place.

Space has been included in the margin of this workbook to use as you see fit for personal notes, recording cash inflow and outflow, recording how you use your time throughout, noting goals or commitments — anything that will help you stay focused on exploring these seven steps of prosperity.

The exercises in this workbook are intended to show you things about yourself, asking you to examine your ideas, beliefs, desires, definitions, and expectations of prosperity. You may find some of the questions and exercises uncomfortable. Don't feel obligated to complete all of them. If an exercise seems too difficult or doesn't feel right to you, skip it for now. Just keep going with the workbook. Later on, you might try going back to any exercise you skipped to see if it works for you now. Examining our core beliefs and patterns can be fascinating and exciting, and at times it can be confrontive. Be sure to be gentle with yourself, not critical.

Using the workbook may bring up issues that you want to discuss with a professional therapist or a support group. A therapist can offer tremendous help and support at certain times in our lives. I always encourage people to get help with particularly difficult issues.

Remember too to have fun and bring a sense of play with you when you work with the concepts, questions, meditations, exercises, and suggestions in this workbook.

The Calendar in the Back

In the back of this workbook, there is a ninety-day calendar. There are several ways you can use this calendar:

1) You may want to attach one of the seven steps to each day of the week to keep you focused on the steps involved in creating true prosperity. You can do morning meditations if you like, in a rotating fashion. Every Sunday, for instance, could be a day of Gratitude; every Monday, a day to focus on Awareness; every Tuesday, a day to envision Healing and Growth; Wednesday, a date with your Intuition; Thursday, a day to meditate on your Vision; Friday, a day to refresh your commitment to your Goals; and Saturday, a day to ponder your connection to others and to Share Your Gifts.

2) You may want to use the calendar to record your spending and receiving, to record exactly how you are spending your time, or to write in your daily goals and commitments. Anything that helps you take action toward more prosperity or reminds you of the prosperity you are experiencing at this moment can be included.

3) You may want to use the calendar to set up a three-month program — or any length of time that feels right for you — to focus on each of the seven steps presented in the workbook. You can also use it in conjunction with certain exercises in the workbook that require a particular time frame or ask you to keep track of things daily, such as the exercise on tracking your money in the Awareness section.

There are many ways to use the calendar provided in the back — it's meant to be a tool — so be creative and have fun with it.

You can also use the sidebars as a calendar if it feels more accessible to you. Date ninety consecutive sidebars (the shaded area at the edge of the page) and use the margin as a place to note commitments to yourself regarding prosperity, to track your time or expenses, or to write a daily affirmation or note the things you are grateful for that particular day.

Setting Your Intention

When beginning any new project, it can be very powerful to set for yourself a clear intention about the results you would like to create. This exercise can help you form a clear intention for using this workbook to help you create a greater experience of true prosperity, whatever that means to you.

Intention Meditation

Find a quiet place and sit or lie down in a comfortable position. Close your eyes and breathe slowly and deeply for a few minutes until your body and mind relax. Let your awareness move into a deep, quiet place inside.

Now imagine that you have been using this workbook for a few weeks or a few months, and you are finding that it is helping you make positive changes in your life. What kinds of changes are happening? Let yourself imagine the changes that you desire, as if they are already happening. Let yourself savor and enjoy the feelings of greater satisfaction and prosperity this brings you.

When you feel complete with this meditation, open your eyes, take a pen, and in whatever words feel right to you, write briefly what you intend to have happen in your life as a result of using this workbook:

- become more balanced with money
- have a debt-free life
- have savings
- not worry about having enough money
- able to buy things for myself and treat others

The purpose of creating an intention is to help us get clear, and to create a powerful momentum in the direction we wish to go. Your intention reflects where you are today. It may change over time. When you finish with the workbook come back and look at your intention again. You may find that you have made progress in this direction, or that your direction has changed entirely. It doesn't matter. You have now begun your journey with this workbook in a powerful way. Enjoy your experience with the workbook. Congratulations on your commitment to yourself!

Gratitude

Whether or not we feel particularly prosperous at this moment, the truth is that most of us in modern western society are enormously prosperous, materially and in many other ways. We need only to compare our lives with the struggle for survival and subsistence that most humans in history have experienced, and that a majority of people in the world today are still experiencing, to realize how truly fortunate we are. Many of us live better than the kings and queens of a few centuries ago.

Take time to acknowledge the prosperity you already have. How many of your needs and desires are already being met? Most of us already have considerable prosperity in our lives. Often, we are so busy pursuing our unmet desires that we are unable to enjoy all that we already have. Allowing ourselves to really appreciate the prosperity we have created is a big step toward opening to even greater fulfillment.

In *Bring in the Blessing Way* Angeles Arrien suggests that if we want what she calls the Blessing Way to come into our lives, we must do three things every day: pray, extend gratitude, and take life-affirming action. In this chapter, we are going to focus on gratitude.

Gratitude List

Write a quick list of everything in your life that you feel especially thankful for at this moment — just whatever comes to your mind first. Add to it whenever you think of something else, or whenever something especially good happens. (Or when something bad happens, and you find a gift in the experience.)

For example:
I am thankful for my sweet little house and my wonderful, private backyard.
I am grateful to have such meaningful, satisfying work.

You can also simply list things rather than writing sentences:

the sun
my relationship with my brother
a reliable car
the use of my hands
having a washer and dryer in the house (even if they squeak)
excellent health

. . . and so on.

You can write more detailed gratitude lists in the individual categories that follow in this section. This quick list is meant to get you thinking about the importance of gratitude in your life.

place to live
car for use
plenty of food
live in a great city
able to train every day
parents
*options
kitties
excellent health
youth
use of my body

Relishing

Whatever our individual troubles and challenges may be (and we all have them) it's important to pause every now and then to appreciate all that we have on every level. We need to literally "count our blessings," give thanks for them, allow ourselves to enjoy them, and relish the experience of prosperity that we already have.

Take five minutes, right now if you can, and relish the level of prosperity you currently have in your life.

TROUBLES AND COMPLAINTS

Sometimes it can be difficult to get in touch with our gratitude because we are feeling so troubled or disappointed about something. If so, it can be helpful to express this, to put it down on paper, and to turn it over to our "higher power" for solution or healing.

So, lay your troubles to rest here. List anything that's troubling you right now.

Ask yourself what's bothering you and list anything that comes up. You may have to take a few breaths, sit quietly, and ask several times.

It might be something that is very apparent and oppressive: *I'm afraid I won't be able to pay next month's rent*, for example.

Or it may be unclear or seem trivial, but keep asking: What's bothering me? *This chair*. What else? *This damp air. I wish it would stop raining*. Try to get a feel for something underneath the discomfort you're feeling: What's *really* bothering me? *Never feeling content, rested, relaxed.*

You may have to go into your body and "feel" your answers if they don't come easily. Pay attention to how your body feels when you ask your questions.

For example, when I am feeling anxious, and not able to quickly understand my anxiety, I start reviewing the last few days and ask myself questions paying attention to how my body reacts to the questions. I know I've stumbled upon what's troubling me when the anxiety increases through my body.

As you continue with the rest of the gratitude exercises, if you feel blocked in a particular area, look to see if there is a problem you need to express. If so, come back to this list and write it down. You can do this any time you need to as you go through the workbook.

TROUBLES AND COMPLAINTS LIST

This is what I'm feeling troubled about right now. In writing it here, I release it, and ask for awareness, understanding, healing, and growth to come in this area of my life.

- I don't have a steady source of income in my life. I want to have freedom from debts and be completely independent. I want to know what I need to do to be able to support myself.

Specific Gratitude Lists

Let's take the gratitude exercise a little further by taking a look at specific areas in our lives. Oftentimes, concentrating on one particular area of your life can unearth new sources of gratitude. So, take some time here to express your appreciation for your life as it is right now in each of the following areas, however humble your list might seem.

Home/Possessions

The things I appreciate about my home and living situation are:

rent-free
nice big house, nobody ever home
my own room
my own bathroom
use of t.v., V.CR, computer, washing machine & dryer.
my own phone
great area
big kitchen
all the utensils & appliances

If there is an object in your home that makes you feel especially prosperous or symbolizes your appreciation for your home, you might want to "use" it as a reminder of the prosperity you already have.

For example, something as simple as a yellow flower in a round, white pot, or family photographs that line the hallway, or a special china tea cup you received as a gift might bring up feelings of luxury and abundance for you. You may choose to focus on this "piece of prosperity" in your life to remind you to stop and say a prayer of gratitude whenever you pass it.

Or, if you want to get really creative, you can sketch, photograph, or otherwise "capture" this object and play with it artistically; then put the art object at eye level in your house, or all over your house. This act lets you immerse yourself in the feelings the object brings up in you, and hanging it where it can be seen can often comfort you and keep you calm.

Work/Career

The things I appreciate about my work situation are:

doing what I love
flexible hours.

Post small notes of gratitude around your computer screen or desk to remind you of the things you appreciate about your work situation. Or, bring fresh flowers to your office, client, or staff member — perhaps even to yourself.

Relationships

I appreciate the following people in my life for the following reasons:

Perhaps you would like to take a break from your workbook and call, write to, or pray for one of them now.

Body/Health/Appearance

I have the following things for which to be grateful in the area of body, health, and appearance:

As part of your morning ritual, take a moment to look in the mirror before you leave for the day, and smile at yourself. Greet yourself with kindness and appreciation.

Myself

I especially like and appreciate these things about myself:

If you are a person who has a difficult time appreciating yourself regularly, you may copy some of what you've written here onto notes and put them on your bathroom mirror where you can see them every day.

Pain

Wait a minute, you're supposed to feel gratitude for pain?! Actually, yes. Remember, every experience in our lives has brought us to where we are today. Painful experiences can be our most powerful teachers.

In what area of your life — relationships, finances, health and appearance, or any other — have you experienced pain that you can see has brought you growth, healing, or wisdom? Here are a few examples of particular areas of painful experience:

Health: *Although I would not have chosen to develop pneumonia, it has prompted me to quit smoking. And, for that, I am grateful. It has shown me how much my friends care for me. It has made me appreciate my warm home, how good a pot of tea can be, and the fact that I have health insurance.*

Relationship: *It would not have been my choice to lose a long-term love relationship, however, I am grateful for the personal growth that has taken place in both our lives and appreciate the relationship as it has moved me toward the person I am today — a person with greater understanding of myself, a person with more compassion, strength, vulnerability, and love.*

Work: *At the time I lost my job I was devastated. However, it did force me to look at what I truly wanted to do with my life and without that "push" I might never have begun the search for my true passion of self-expression and service in the world.*

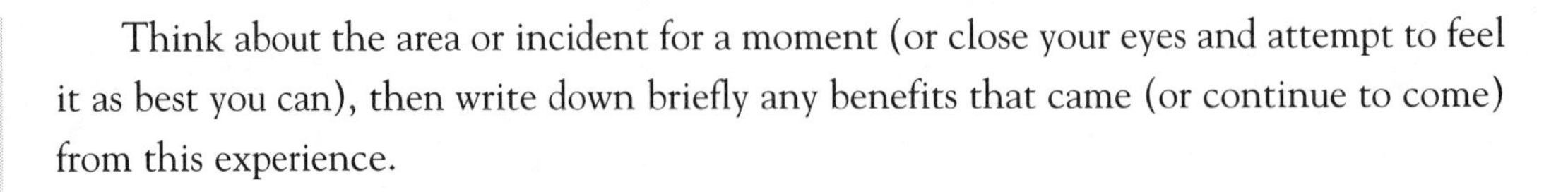

Think about the area or incident for a moment (or close your eyes and attempt to feel it as best you can), then write down briefly any benefits that came (or continue to come) from this experience.

I have the following things for which to be grateful in the area of pain:

Miscellaneous Gratitude (For anything that hasn't yet been covered.)

I am grateful for the following things in my life:

Daily Appreciation Exercise

When you wake up each morning or before going to sleep at night, take a minute or two to think about the things you appreciate in your life. If you are feeling troubled about something, there's no need to brush that aside. Acknowledge that feeling as well, and remind yourself that you are willing to learn and benefit from every experience in your life.

You may not be able to do this appreciation exercise every day, but remembering to do it as often as possible will enormously expand your experience of prosperity, and create space for more to come.

Enough Is Enough

One thing that can interfere with our experience of prosperity is an underlying fear of never having enough. We can unwittingly be repeating to ourselves, day after day, year after year, "I don't have enough time. I don't have enough money. I don't have enough love." You may come across these fears or others as you do exercises in the Awareness and Healing and Growth sections of this workbook. For now, read the following statements out loud. Feel free to add anything else that you feel deprived of. As you read these words, imagine that they are true. Experience the possibility of them being true, if only for a moment.

I have enough time. I have enough money. I have enough love.

If it feels good to you, say these affirmations to yourself throughout the day, whenever you notice yourself tightening up with the fear of not having enough.

EXPRESSING APPRECIATION EXERCISE

Make it a practice to express your appreciation as often as possible — especially to the people in your life who enhance your experience of prosperity. Let them know in your own words and deeds how much they mean to you. Make a small commitment toward expression here:

I would like to express my appreciation to:

I will express my gratitude this week by:

I want to thank myself for:

"SPEECH! SPEECH!"

This is a little exercise to encourage the expression of gratitude for yourself and others in your life. Pretend you are accepting your Academy Award for being who you are today. Enjoy it. After all, you don't get too many Academy Awards in a lifetime. Write your acceptance speech below.

Meditation / Being Appreciated

Imagine yourself in some everyday situation, and picture someone (maybe someone you know, or a stranger) looking at you with great love and admiration and telling you something he or she really likes about you. Now picture a few more people coming up and agreeing that you are a very wonderful person. (If this embarrasses you, stick with it.) Imagine more and more people arriving and gazing at you with tremendous love and respect in their eyes. Picture yourself in a parade or on a stage, with throngs of cheering, applauding people, all loving and appreciating you. Hear their applause ringing in your ears. Stand up and take a bow, and thank them for their support and appreciation.

Awareness

We all have certain ideas, attitudes, core beliefs, and emotional patterns that either support or limit our experience of prosperity. Deep feelings of unworthiness, a sense of scarcity, fear of failure or success, conflicting feelings and beliefs about money, and other issues can block our growth and fulfillment.

Most of these beliefs and patterns are initially unconscious; we are not really aware of them and yet they control our lives. The moment we begin to consciously recognize them, we are on the road to having a real choice about how we live.

Becoming aware of what doesn't work in how we are living is by far the most powerful step in our growth. It is also the most difficult and uncomfortable. As soon as we recognize a problem, we are on the road to healing it. However, that healing takes time. Meanwhile, we may have to watch ourselves repeat the same old patterns a few more times.

As we become more aware, we may be tempted to criticize ourselves for repeating self-defeating patterns, or not advancing quickly enough. It is important to understand how powerful awareness is. When we are unconscious, we will repeat a particular behavior endlessly without gaining much benefit. Once we have some awareness we can catch ourself repeating the same old behavior and learn an enormous amount. We may really feel the pain of it. Then, we are motivated to explore other possible ways of handling the same situation. It's not long before things start to change. Focus on gaining awareness, and change will follow.

Every event of our lives is part of this process, and every experience, with the help of awareness, can contribute to our personal growth and the development of a greater sense of true prosperity.

Mirroring

Everything in our lives reflects our consciousness. Our beliefs, attitudes, expectations, feelings, and emotional patterns are all mirrored in the circumstances and events of our lives. For example, if I am very critical of myself, I'm likely to attract and be attracted to people who mirror that internal process by being critical of me as well. The more I love and support myself emotionally, the more likely I am to attract loving, supportive behavior from others. If I feel that life offers me few opportunities, I'm likely to find that to be true in reality. If I have confidence in my abilities, on the other hand, I will probably discover many opportunities to use them.

Most of us have at least one aspect of our lives where we feel stuck, where we have problems, or where we just seem to repeat the same unsatisfying patterns over and over again. Whenever we have difficulties like this, life is reflecting that this is an area where we need increased awareness, healing, and development.

Our lives are incredible mirrors. They show us exactly what steps we need to take in our personal growth at any given moment. We just have to learn to pay attention to these messages.

Our experience of prosperity will develop as a reflection of our increasing awareness and healing in all areas of our lives.

In this section of the workbook, there are many exercises that may help you gain a greater awareness of your ideas, beliefs, feelings, and patterns related to prosperity as well as how you spend your financial resources. These exercises may also help you gain insight about how your inner feelings and beliefs are being reflected in your life in various ways.

Being Aware of Our Beliefs about Prosperity

Let's examine some of our ideas, beliefs, and attitudes concerning money and prosperity. Some of the questions and exercises in this section may give you some insight into the prosperity-related issues at your core. Take this opportunity to begin (or continue) to examine some of your beliefs about money, power, and prosperity.

Complete the following sentences quickly and spontaneously with whatever comes to mind. Try not to "edit" yourself; just write down whatever comes to you. It's okay if it's somewhat repetitive.

Feel free to let your answer take any form: it may be an essay or a spontaneous poem, anything, as long as you are attempting to define prosperity for yourself as you respond.

Prosperity is:

Prosperity is:

Prosperity is:

Prosperity is:

Abundance means:

Abundance means:

Abundance means:

Abundance means:

Wealth is:

Wealth is:

Wealth is:

Wealth is:

Affluence means:

Affluence means:

Affluence means:

Affluence means:

You can use the following pages to continue this exercise by writing your definition of the following prosperity-related terms. Again, use any form you wish — words, poems, prose, even drawings.

riches	fortune	treasure
cash	assets	property
money	means	capital
resources	revenue	currency
munificence	copiousness	bounty
fertility	plenty	generosity

Surviving and Thriving

What are your ideas about the difference between someone who is surviving and someone who is thriving in life? Write about this:

AWARENESS OF OUR BELIEFS ABOUT MONEY

As we have seen, prosperity isn't caused by money. In the modern world, however, most of us have a lifestyle in which we deal with money. Our finances are one important *aspect* of our prosperity. So if we want to experience prosperity, we have to look at our relationship to money, and understand what it can teach us.

Essentially, money is a symbol for energy. It is a medium of exchange we have chosen to represent our creative energy. Money itself just consists of a piece of paper or metal (or these days, plastic) with little intrinsic value, but we have chosen to let it symbolize the energy we exchange with one another.

Since money symbolizes energy, our financial affairs tend to reflect how our life energy is moving. When we are living our truth, following the flow of life, usually our finances also flow freely. If our energy is blocked, frequently our money is too. Money is just another mirror that reveals what is going on in our consciousness.

Money can represent many things to us: security, power, freedom, validation, success, temptation, evil, to name a few. Our financial circumstances may reflect how we feel about the qualities we consciously or unconsciously associate with money. Since money reflects energy, it is drawn to those who respect and welcome it, and is repelled by those who view it with fear or dislike.

The following writing exercises will help you further examine your beliefs about money.

Money Exercise

Take a look at the financial circumstances surrounding you at birth, both in terms of your immediate family, and in terms of the community and society in which your family lived. Was it a prosperous time for your family and community, a time of financial struggle and deprivation, or somewhere in between? What were your first impressions of money and prosperity? Write a description of whatever you remember or know about this:

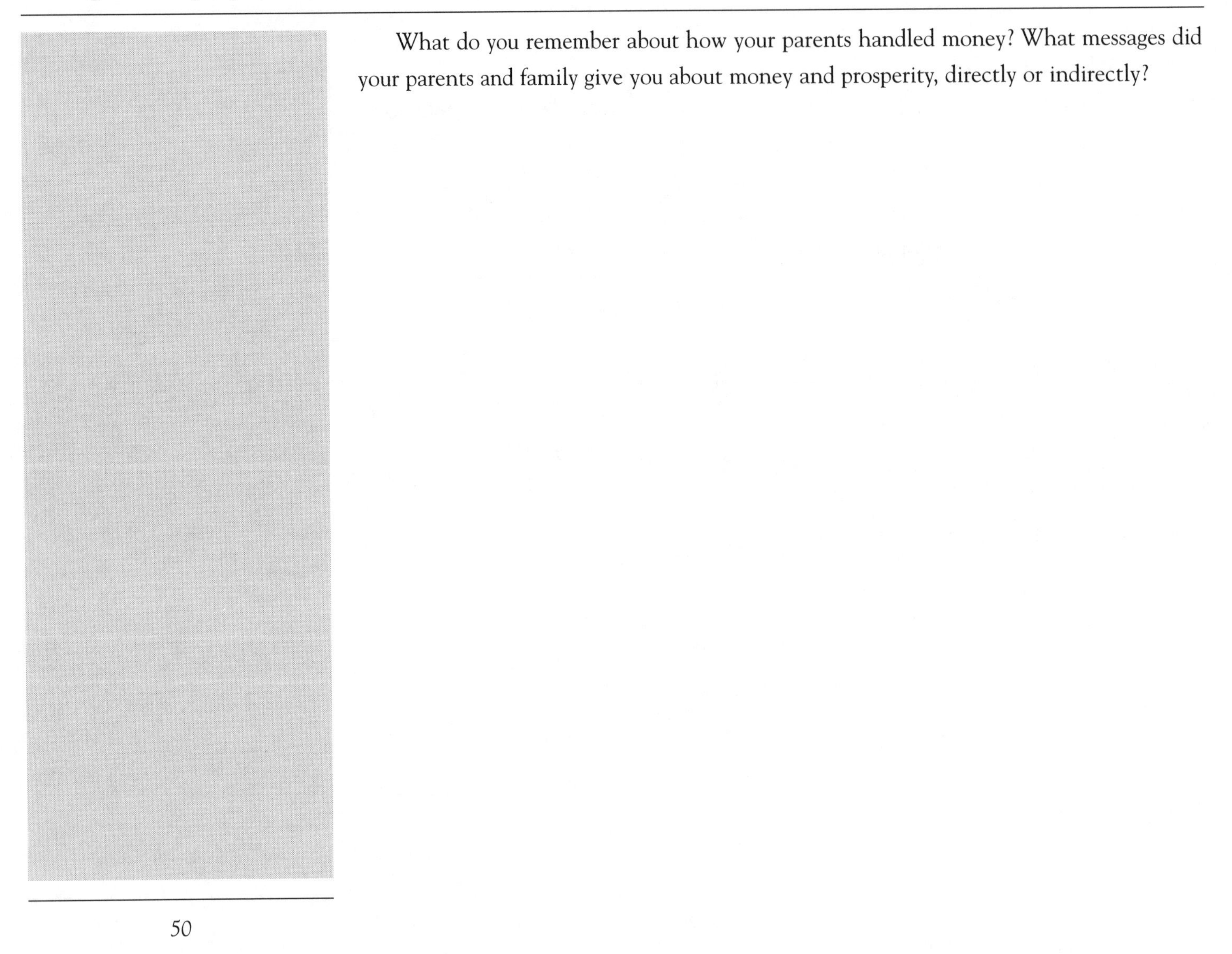

What do you remember about how your parents handled money? What messages did your parents and family give you about money and prosperity, directly or indirectly?

Do you remember any traumatic experiences related to money or prosperity in your early life? Write a brief description of these incidents. How did they affect your feelings and beliefs about prosperity?

In what ways are you still being influenced, reacting to, or acting out these early experiences; and how is that affecting your experience of prosperity?

In what ways would you like to change your beliefs and feelings about money and prosperity?

Awareness of Our Beliefs about Power

To understand our relationship with money, it is important to recognize that money gives us power in the world. Having money allows us to do things, to get things, and to make things happen.

Our relationship with money reflects how we feel about our power to have an effect on the world. The more comfortable we are with being powerful, the more money we are likely to create in our lives.

Many of us have issues with power, and these are likely to be reflected in our relationship with money. In fact, if you have chronic financial problems, I strongly suggest that you take a deep honest look at your feelings about power.

If we have issues about power, we generally relate to money by either pursuing or avoiding it. If we crave power, we may pursue money as a way of gaining that power. However, a yearning for power is really a way that we compensate for a fundamental feeling of powerlessness. We may be driven by the unconscious desire to avoid our deep feelings of fear and helplessness. No amount of money will ever be enough to take away the fear that is unconsciously held at the emotional level. Only by consciously acknowledging our fear and vulnerability can we begin the healing process that leads to a true feeling of abundance.

If we are afraid of our power, we may unconsciously keep ourselves from having very much money, since to have money is to have power. In fact, struggling with a financial lack is an effective way to keep ourselves feeling powerless, and thereby avoid the risks we may associate with having power.

If we have had early life experiences of being physically or emotionally abused by someone with power, or if we have witnessed someone misusing power, we may be deeply imprinted with a fear of power. On one hand, we may be afraid that if we become too visible (successful in the world) we will be noticed and abused again. We equate being seen with being unsafe. At the same time, we may fear that if we allow ourselves to become powerful, we will also abuse that power. Unconsciously, we may prefer to remain powerless and struggling rather than take the risk that power may be corruptive or harmful.

Obviously, these fears have some validity, and cannot be pushed aside or ignored. They must be acknowledged and worked with. A key thing to realize is that we need not go to extremes. We cannot become completely swept up in worldly power, nor can we deny and disown our personal power; we need to find a balance.

Here is one pattern I've often encountered: If we weren't cared for in the ways we really needed to be as a child, that child part of us still lives within us and still yearns to be taken care of by a parent. The child inside, which we are usually unconscious of, feels that if we grow up and become independent and successful, it will forever lose the opportunity to be cared for. Even though we may consciously wish to succeed, the inner child may sabotage any chance for success and power in the world because it feels it will never receive the nurturing and love it craves. Instead, a pattern of failing develops. This is fueled by the unconscious hope that someday someone will come along and take care of us. This desire is not a bad thing; it's understandable, but we need to bring it into our conscious awareness.

If we become aware of these unconscious patterns, we can begin to heal them.*

---

*For guidance on healing your inner child, I recommend *Recovery of Your Inner Child* by Lucia Capacchione, and *Notes from My Inner Child* by Tanha Luvaas.

Power Exercise

Here is an exercise taken from the book, *Creating True Prosperity*, to help you further examine your feelings about power and how they might be affecting your relationship with financial prosperity. New questions have been added, and even if you have done this exercise before, you may want to ask yourself again, possibly even regularly for a certain period of time. Your answers may change over time.

Trust your initial responses and try not to think too much when you answer the questions. There are no right or wrong answers, and you can answer them again tomorrow, if you like. This exercise is designed to help you gain an awareness of your beliefs about power. Be honest and have fun.

If I get too powerful I might:

If I get too powerful I might not:

My mother thinks power is:

My father thinks power is:

I think powerful people are:

A powerful woman is:

A powerful man is:

The advantage of not being powerful is:

If I were wealthy and successful, I would:

If I were wealthy and successful, I wouldn't:

The last time I felt powerful was:

I feel a sense of power when I am:

What feelings came up as a result of answering the above questions? Did any of your answers surprise you or give you particular insight into your beliefs about power? Record any comments below:

Power Day Exercise

This exercise is intended to increase your awareness of how you feel with regard to power.

Choose a day within the next week to call your "power" day. Begin your day by saying the affirmations that follow, or some of your own choosing. You may want to choose only one or two so they can be easily remembered. Repeat these regularly throughout the day (perhaps even every hour or two) to bring your awareness back to power. Remember that power can take many different forms and expressions — physical, mental, emotional, or spiritual. Notice which forms of power come easily to you, and which are difficult or unfamiliar.

Allow yourself to experience the entire day as a powerful person to the best of your ability. Note any resistance that comes up each time you do this, including feelings or events that seem to restrict you from feeling powerful — interactions with certain people, for instance. Even if you spend the entire day noticing how often you feel powerless, it will be time well spent. The point is to bring about an awareness of how you feel with regard to power, not to berate yourself for a lack of power or poor use of it. Be gentle with yourself.

Power Affirmations

It is natural to be powerful.
My power is good.
I accept that I am a powerful person.
I am comfortable with my power.
My power enhances my attractiveness.
I use my power to accomplish my goals and express my purpose in life.

Power Day Notes

Write down any struggles or triumphs that you encounter in the course of your Power Day.

Critical Voices

Sometimes a good place to start freeing up your awareness is the place of most resistance. It is important to acknowledge and honor all our feelings and beliefs.

We all have conflicting voices inside of us. It's important to notice and recognize these voices and give them a chance for expression.

So, let's get negative and talk about money. Tune into that voice of discontent — the Critic, the Whiner — whatever character name best describes the aspect(s) of you that resists all this talk about awareness and prosperity. Express your most negative feelings about money, prosperity, and power in the space below.

This is what I think about money:

This is what I think about power:

This is what I believe will happen if I become a prosperous person:

When you feel you have exhausted the negative possibilities, shift your point of view to a more "positive" aspect of yourself and answer the same questions.

This is what I think about money:

This is what I think about power:

This is what I believe will happen if I become a more prosperous person:

Giving different aspects of yourself the freedom to express themselves without fear of being judged will go a long way toward increasing your sense of prosperity. Keep in mind that prosperity is primarily an experience of what we truly want. Expanding your awareness of the aspects of you in conflict (or aspects with competing desires), will help you take steps toward resolution. The more we learn to accept and express all aspects of who we are, the more freedom, satisfaction, and wholeness we experience, and the more prosperous we feel. We will work with this more in the Healing and Growth section of the workbook.

Money Awareness

There is another aspect of awareness that is an important key to increasing both our financial prosperity and our overall experience of well-being. We need to have a very clear and precise awareness of how money flows in our lives. To put it simply, we need to know where it comes from and where it goes. In order to know this, we need to pay attention and keep track of it.

This might seem obvious to some people. However, many of us strongly resist this step. We have only a vague sense of how the money comes and where it goes. We don't want to confront this reality too closely because we're afraid we won't like what we find out. We may tell ourselves that we don't have to deal with all that dry, boring, financial stuff. Perhaps we have a spouse or someone else in our lives that handles that for us. Or we simply trust that the universe will take care of us if we don't worry about it.

Unfortunately, in the long run, this attitude can undermine our ability to prosper. When we are unaware of the realities of money, we remain somewhat ungrounded in the material world. On a deep level, we feel unsettled and insecure. We may give our power away to another person to take care of us in this realm. This puts us in a very dependent position, which can be quite disempowering. It can be bewildering or even disastrous if that person dies, leaves, or turns out to be untrustworthy.

Having a clear awareness about the movement of money in our lives and learning how to manage it effectively gives us a certain feeling of groundedness, stability, and power that contributes greatly to our overall sense of well-being.

If we want to attract money into our lives, we have to like and respect it, which means not being afraid to get to know it and relate to it.

The following exercise is the first basic step anyone needs to take in order to become aware of how and where money is flowing in his or her life. If you already keep track of your money and have great clarity about your income and expenses, you can choose to skip this exercise. However, I suggest that you go ahead and do it, as you may be surprised at what you discover!

Once you have become more aware of the coming and going of money in your life, the next step is to learn to manage it more effectively. We will touch on this in the Healing and Growth section of this workbook. For a much more thorough look at this topic, I highly recommend two excellent books: *The Money Drunk: 90 Days to Financial Freedom* by Mark Bryan and Julia Cameron, for those who struggle with chronic financial difficulties and debts, and *The Nine Steps to Financial Freedom* by Suze Orman. For everyone!

Tracking Your Money

Buy a notebook small enough to keep with your wallet, in your pocket or purse. Write in it every single penny you spend right when you spend it. Write the date, the amount, what it was for, and whether it was paid with cash, a check, or a credit card. Also write down every bit of income you receive — the date, the amount, and the source.

Example:

Income	April 27 Expenses	Source
$975.00 — paycheck	$127.00 — groceries	check
$2.75 — refund	$1.25 — coffee	cash
	.50 — daughter's bus fare	cash
	$83.67 — clothes	credit card
	$312.42 — dental bill	check

If you forget to do this at some point, just start again with the next income or expense. Do this for at least three months. This will begin to give you a basic idea of where your money comes from and where it goes. A year is even better, since there are certain expenses, such as insurance, or income such as bonuses, that may occur on an annual or semi-annual basis.

This exercise may be confrontive for some of you, or may seem silly or boring. It may bring out the "rebellious child" in you who doesn't want to do it. It's up to you of course, but if you do choose to do it I think you will find it very empowering in the long run.

After you've done this exercise for a month, create general categories for each type of income and expense that you have. Then add up the income you have in each category, and your total income for the month. Add up the expenses in each category, and your total expenses for the month.

As you track your money in this way, you may realize that you are spending more than you earn, especially if you are using credit cards. Don't panic. That's pretty common. At least now you can begin to understand why your debt keeps adding up, or why you always feel slightly "behind."

You may notice some interesting things about your spending habits. For example, you might notice that you spend a lot of money eating out, yet seldom buy yourself an item of clothing. Becoming aware of your patterns may give you clues about bringing more balance into your life, and make you think about your priorities.

If you are spending more than you earn, it's time to start thinking creatively about how to earn more or spend less. Is there a way you can earn more, without undue stress? Stay open to possibilities you may not have thought of. How could you cut down on some of your expenses? Don't think in terms of major deprivation and sacrifice. Think about taking a little bit off in several categories. There's always a way to make things work, so be open to finding what that might be.

If you can't fully pay off your credit card bills every month, I strongly recommend that you stop using them immediately, if possible. They are the biggest culprits in most people's financial messes.

In this process, try not to be judgmental about yourself. You are gathering information here that can help you create a more prosperous life. Appreciate yourself for having the courage to do this.

While you are in the process of tracking your money, continue through the workbook.

The knowledge you are gaining about your money habits will intermingle with what you learn from the other exercises to increase your overall awareness, and open you to greater prosperity.

Simplifying Your Life

Your first thought may be, *I can't simplify my life* — but this is probably not true. If you believe it is impossible to simplify your life, you will not give yourself the opportunity to explore the possibilities. So assume, for the moment, that you *can* simplify your life.

Go back to the beginning of the workbook where you wrote the things that are most important to you. Review the day ahead of you, everything you have planned. Is there anything that conflicts with what you've labeled as important to you?

Most of us think we want to simplify our lives, but when it comes down to it, we are unwilling to make changes!

Is there anything that you do out of obligation rather than from true desire? Social events, perhaps? Can you trust that others — coworkers, friends, family — want you to do what's best for you, which in some cases means declining invitations?

Are there some boundaries you can set for yourself and with others to allow for more focused work or creative endeavors?

Can you get the most difficult task of the day out of your way early?

Every situation is unique. For one person, simplifying might mean hiring help around the house, while for another it might mean dismissing hired help in order to lower the cost of living.

There are many books available that address the challenge of simplifying your life. I would encourage anyone interested to take a look at some of these.

Simplifying Your Life Exercise

You can take steps to simplify your life almost immediately. One way of doing this is to make a list of things that overwhelm you and come up with alternative ways to handle them. Keep in mind, however, that simplifying means different things to different people. For example, you might say that keeping up with your weekly household chores is overwhelming. An alternative way to handle this would be to cut back on your office hours in order to give you more time at home to take care of these chores; another alternative would be to keep your office hours and hire someone to come into your home one or two days a week to keep up with the chores for you.

Keep it simple, this exercise is not meant to overwhelm you.

Overwhelming items	Alternative Ways to Handle

Awareness Meditation

Sit or lie down in a comfortable position. Close your eyes. What are you aware of right now? Just notice anything that comes into your awareness, whether it be sounds from your surrounding environment, sensations in your body, your thoughts, your emotions, or whatever. Every time you find yourself getting lost in a thought and drifting off, gently bring your attention back into your present place and time, becoming aware of whatever is "here." Don't attempt to do anything, change anything, understand anything. Stay as present as you can, and simply be aware of whatever you notice. You may find that your mind is racing throughout the exercise. Or you may find that you grow quieter and more relaxed. It doesn't matter what happens, just practice being aware of whatever you are experiencing. Do this for ten or fifteen minutes (more if you like).

If you do this exercise regularly, it will greatly expand your ability to be aware of what is happening inside you and around you. And you'll discover many other benefits from this simple form of meditation as well.

Healing & Growth

As we gain greater awareness, a tremendous amount of healing and growth takes place in our lives. We begin to heal old wounds, attitudes, and patterns that no longer serve us. We get more in touch with our own essence, and begin to develop and express ourselves in new ways.

Life is always attempting to move us in the direction of our own evolution and development. This takes place in many different ways. In fact, every experience and event of our lives contributes to our growth. Once we become aware of the fact that life is one big learning experience, it's easier to cooperate with the process. We can actively support and participate in our own healing and growth. Every step we take along our path adds to our experience of true prosperity.

Fortunately, we live in a time when there are many tools, techniques, teachers, guides, and mentors to help us along the way. Of course, some are better than others, and some are right for us at one time in our lives and not at another. It is important to choose carefully who we allow to influence us. Remember that everyone has his or her human flaws and limitations, even the most seemingly evolved or enlightened.

We can learn much and receive considerable support from others, as long as we don't give our power away to anyone else. It is essential to keep the ultimate authority within ourselves.

The Four Levels of Human Life

In order for us to experience the greatest sense of prosperity, the work of healing needs to be done on all levels of our existence: the spiritual, mental, emotional, and physical. In order to find balance, wholeness, and fulfillment in our lives, we need to heal, develop, and integrate all four of these aspects within ourselves.

Spiritual

Our spiritual aspect is our inner essence, our soul, the part of us that exists beyond time and space. It connects us with the universal source and the oneness of life. Developing our awareness of the spiritual level of our being allows us to experience a feeling of "belonging" in the universe, a deeper meaning and purpose in our lives, and a broader perspective than we have from our personality alone. The spiritual level provides a foundation for the development of the other levels.

Mental

Our mental aspect is our intellect, our ability to think and reason. The mental level of our existence consists of our thoughts, attitudes, beliefs, and values. Developing the mental level of our being allows us to think clearly, remain open-minded, yet discriminate intelligently. Our minds enable us to gather knowledge and wisdom from our life experience and from the world around us.

Emotional

Our emotional aspect is our ability to experience life deeply, to relate to one another and the world on a feeling level. It's the part of us that seeks meaningful contact and connection with others. Developing the emotional level of our being allows us to feel the full range of the human experience, and find fulfillment in our relationships with ourselves and each other.

Physical

Our physical aspect is, of course, our physical body. It also includes our ability to survive and thrive in the material world. Developing the physical level of our being involves learning to take good care of our bodies, and to enjoy them. It also means developing the skills to live comfortably and effectively in the world.

All four of these levels of existence are equally important. In the long run, we can't afford to neglect any of them. If we want to feel whole and lead healthy, satisfying lives, we need to focus a certain amount of time and attention on healing and developing each aspect.

Assessing the Four Levels

Take a few minutes to think about which of the four aspects you have developed and which one(s) might need more healing and expression in your life. In the following exercise, write how you experience each of the four levels in your life at this time. Take

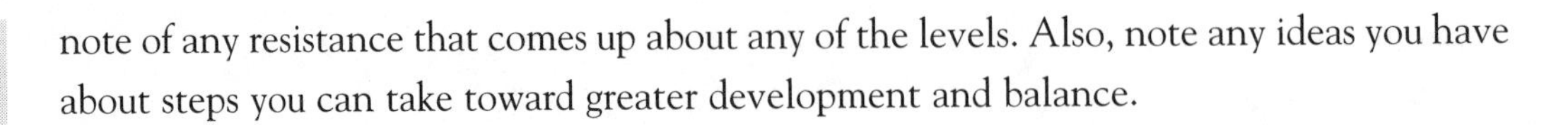
note of any resistance that comes up about any of the levels. Also, note any ideas you have about steps you can take toward greater development and balance.

Physical

Are you physically healthy and active? Do you like and feel comfortable in your body? Do you enjoy your sexuality? Are you comfortable in the material world? Are you practical, down to earth, financially stable?

Do you sense any resistance or blocks within you that might keep you from further developing the physical aspect of your life? If so, what are they? What would you need to do to open the way for further development of this area?

What steps could you take toward enhancing your relationship with your physical self and the material world?

Emotional

Are you in touch with your feelings and are you able to express them appropriately? Do you allow yourself to feel the full range of emotions — fear, sadness, anger, as well as love and joy — or do you find that certain emotions make you uncomfortable? Are you able to set appropriate boundaries with people? Can you relate to others in a close, intimate way?

Is there any resistance within you toward allowing yourself to feel certain emotions? Do you have difficulty taking good care of yourself emotionally? What would help?

What steps could you take toward healing and balancing the emotional aspect of your life?

Mental

Are you satisfied with your intellect? Can you think and express yourself clearly? Do you have a belief system that supports you and works for you? Are you open to new ideas without being overly impressionable?

Do you have anything that's blocking you from mental clarity or development? Do you resist examining your belief systems, or entertaining new ideas?

What steps could you take to enhance the mental aspect of your life?

Spiritual

Do you feel a sense of connection to your spiritual source? Are you able to spend time quiet and alone, just "being"? Do you have a relationship with your own inner wisdom and intuitive guidance? Do you have moments when you feel at one with everything or part of some greater whole?

Does anything block you or stop you from connecting with your spiritual essence?

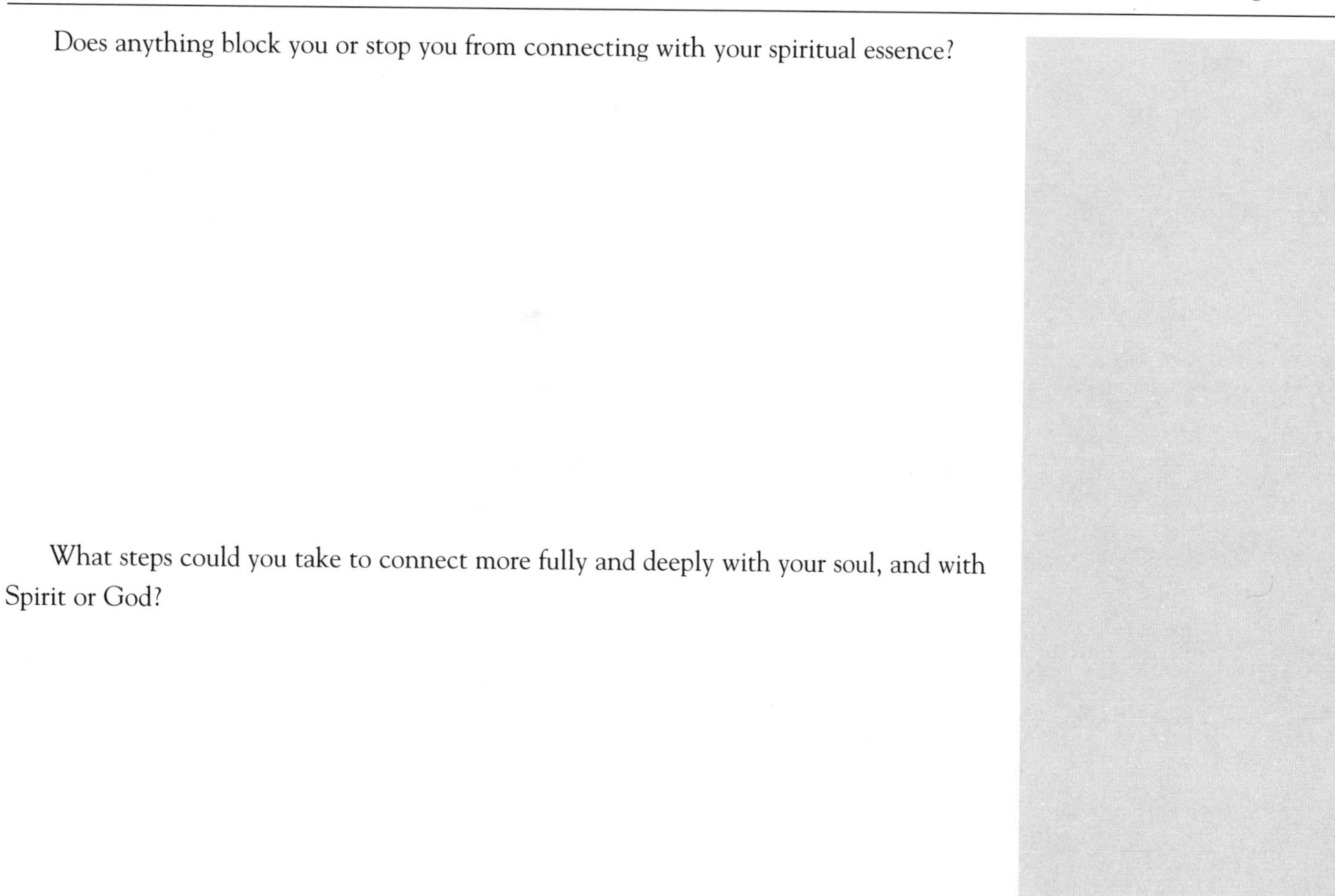

What steps could you take to connect more fully and deeply with your soul, and with Spirit or God?

You might find one or two of these areas stand out as needing your attention, or you may feel that all four aspects need a little tuning up. Perhaps you will find that you are already very developed and balanced on all levels.

Rather than approaching the four levels of healing as a goal to be reached as quickly as possible so we achieve some ideal state of balance, we need to understand that this is an ongoing, ever-unfolding journey. We need to have great patience, compassion, and acceptance of ourselves in the process.

As we follow our healing path, giving our attention to each of the levels as the need arises, we find that all four aspects — spiritual, mental, emotional, and physical — gradually become more integrated with one another. If we learn to pay attention, our own inner intuitive guidance will show us each step we need to take along the way, and we will increasingly come into greater balance and harmony.

For a deeper understanding of how the healing of each of these aspects affect our lives, refer to my book *The Four Levels of Healing*.

Four Levels Meditation

Here is a meditation to help you integrate all four levels. This is a good one to do on a daily or regular basis.

Sit or lie down in a comfortable position with your back straight and supported. Close your eyes and relax. Take a deep breath, and as you exhale, let go of everything you don't need to focus on right now. Take another deep breath, and as you exhale, let your awareness move deep inside. Keep breathing slowly and fully, and allow your attention to move deeper and deeper until you come to a quiet place inside.

In this quiet place, open to feeling and experiencing your spiritual essence. Just sit quietly and invite your spirit in. Whether or not you feel anything in particular, assume it's there. Know that it is always with you at every moment of your life. In this place, you are one with all of creation.

Now move slowly to the mental level. Imagine yourself mentally very clear and alert. Imagine that you believe in yourself; you have confidence in your power to create and manifest whatever you truly want in your life. You believe that life is supporting you in every way.

Now check in with yourself on the emotional level. How are you feeling right now? Can you accept and be with your feelings? Imagine yourself feeling comfortable with all your emotions. Know that as human beings we have many deep feelings that are gifts to help us take care of ourselves, to teach us about life. So imagine yourself respecting and honoring all your feelings and learning to express them appropriately and constructively.

Become aware of your physical body, and sense how it is feeling. Give your body the love and appreciation it deserves. Imagine that you are learning to listen to your body and pay attention to what it needs and feels. You take good care of it, and as a result it feels healthy, fit, alive, and beautiful. Imagine feeling comfortable and happy in your body.

Now expand that feeling to your surroundings. Imagine yourself feeling comfortable and confident in the physical world, able to take good care of yourself and handle the practical aspects of life easily and efficiently. Your environment reflects this — it is orderly and beautiful. Take a few minutes to imagine your day unfolding in a flowing and fulfilling way.

When you feel complete with this, slowly open your eyes, stretch gently, and go about your life.

Developing Balance and Integration

Now that we have explored the four main aspects of human life, let's turn our attention to working with the many energies within us. This section of the workbook focuses on ways to do this.

The physical world is a plane of duality. Life on earth contains an infinite number of polarities. For every truth, there is an equal and opposite truth. Every energy has a corresponding opposite.

Each one of us is a microcosm of the universe; that is, we are born with all the energies and archetypes of life potentially within us. One of the greatest challenges in our personal evolution is to develop and integrate into our lives as many of these energies as possible. The more aspects of ourselves that we discover and learn to express, the more fullness, wholeness, and prosperity we experience. In order to do this, we must learn to embrace and balance life's polarities. Let's look at an example of a pair of opposite energies within us.

Power and Vulnerability

Every one of us is innately powerful. We are born with potential power; our task is to claim it, develop it, and become comfortable with expressing it in our own unique way. At the same time, we are all innately vulnerable. As human beings, we have needs and feelings that cause us to be deeply sensitive. We all must learn sooner or later to become comfortable with our vulnerability — to acknowledge it and take the responsibility to care for it.

Power and vulnerability are opposite energies. Our power is our ability to affect the world around us. Our vulnerability is our ability to be affected by the world around us. To have a rich, full, and successful experience of life, we need to embrace both these polarities. One of the great challenges of the human experience is to learn to live with this paradox: We are both extremely powerful and extremely vulnerable. There are many similar paradoxes that require us to accept all aspects of ourselves. True healing lies in this self-acceptance.

This way of looking at life is quite different than the viewpoint most of us are familiar with. In modern Western culture, we have a very linear, polarized approach to the dualities of life. Instead of seeing them holistically — as equally valuable aspects of a greater whole — we view them as good or bad, right or wrong. From this perspective, we feel we must *choose between* opposites rather than honoring both. We are constantly trying to determine which side of any polarity is correct, good, true, or better. We then support and develop that side while attempting to get rid of its opposite, which we think is bad or wrong.

Not only does this lead to judging ourselves and others, but it ensures we will be in continual conflict within ourselves. Since all of life's energies are innate and essential, we can't get rid of any of them no matter how hard we might try. When we attempt to choose one quality over another, we start an internal war (which, incidentally, is reflected by all the wars we create in the external world).*

Let's look at the polarities we discussed — power and vulnerability. In our society, power is generally honored and respected, while vulnerability is judged as weak, embarrassing, and shameful. Because of this cultural bias, most of us attempt to develop our power in one way or another, and eradicate, or at least hide, our vulnerability. This is especially true for men, because the traditional bias against vulnerability in men is enormous.

*For more information on this, refer to my book *The Path of Transformation*.

The problem with this stance is that as humans we simply are vulnerable. Trying to overcome this fact will not make it go away. At best, we learn to hide it from ourselves and others, which leaves us living in denial. Even sadder, we are attempting to rid ourselves of an essential ingredient to a satisfying life. Our vulnerability is the doorway to our receptivity; without it we cannot receive love, we cannot experience intimacy, we cannot find fulfillment.

People who are overly identified with power and deny their vulnerability may be able to accomplish a great deal. But they will not really be able to receive life's spiritual and emotional rewards, and ultimately may wonder what the point of life is.

Despite our cultural preference for power, many people consciously or unconsciously choose an opposite path in life. If we've had a damaging experience in our early life with someone who misused power, we may attempt to disown our power. We may identify with vulnerability out of fear that our power might be perceived as a threat or might actually hurt people. Unfortunately, this approach is just as lopsided in an opposite way.

Without our power, we cannot accomplish our goals in life, or share our gifts, or properly protect and care for ourselves. A person who is overly identified with vulnerability often becomes a victim of other people or of life's circumstances.

As we discussed previously, overidentification with either power or vulnerability often causes some kind of problem with money and prosperity. If we're identified with power, we may pursue money to the exclusion of other important things. If we're identified with vulnerability and disown our power, we may block ourselves from making money or achieving success.

Honoring All Energies

Attempting to choose between the polarities of life — judging certain qualities as "good" or "positive" and others as "bad" or "negative" — causes us to become imbalanced in ways that ultimately become quite painful and frustrating.

Life is always confronting us with the ways that we are lopsided, and nudging — or outright pushing — us in the direction of greater balance. If you are overly identified with power, you may develop an ailment, or lose a relationship or loved one — forcing you to acknowledge and make peace with your vulnerability. If you disown your power, life may force you into a position where you have to stand up for your beliefs, or where you are called on in some way to find your strength.

The key here is this: We must learn to honor all the energies of life. We must understand that for every truth there is an equal and opposite truth. When confronted with a set of polarities — rationality and intuition, for example — we must recognize the value on both sides and somehow grow enough to embrace it all. Once we can make friends with all aspects of ourselves, we have access to our full repertoire of energies. This allows us to approach life's various challenges and experiences much more creatively and appropriately than when we are stuck in rigid roles.

What about the fact that certain energies truly seem negative? For example, if you are a very hardworking person, you might consider the opposite of hard work to be laziness. You might think, *What could be the value in laziness and why would I honor that? Obviously, hard work is good and laziness is bad!* In order to understand this, you have to look underneath the judgmental words you use to describe this polarity. What is the essential quality underneath the judgmental word "lazy"? If you drop the judgment, you might find that quality is "being able to relax." Is it possible that as a hardworking person, you could benefit from a greater ability to relax? If so, you must first honor that quality, and acknowledge its value for you.

Remember that we are talking about balance. The idea is not to throw anything out, but to find the appropriate balance of energies that can help you live your life in a more satisfying manner.

This is not a simple concept; embracing the opposites within us requires awareness and understanding. Perhaps the diagrams below and on the next page can help to make this clearer. The first one is an example of how we may have thought about certain opposites.

The second one shows the holistic, inclusive perspective — note that the opposites are contained within the whole.

DIAGRAM ONE: JUDGMENTAL VIEW

POSITIVE QUALITIES	NEGATIVE QUALITIES
Qualities I want	*Qualities I don't want*
Hardworking	Lazy
Strong	Weak
Caring	Selfish
Responsible	Irresponsible
Rational	Irrational
Organized	Chaotic

Diagram Two: Inclusive View

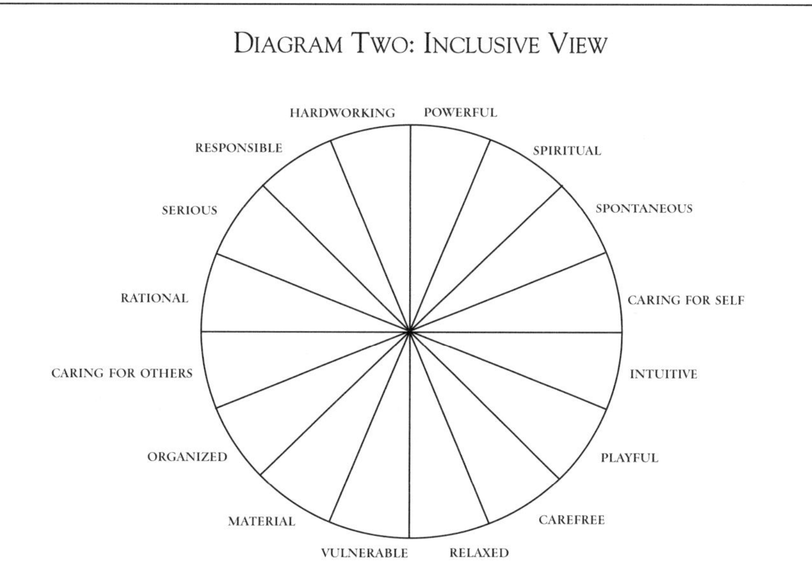

This is all part of who I am.
I need and want all of these qualities.

What does this have to do with prosperity? Everything! Remember, prosperity is primarily an experience. When we are out of balance — overly identified with certain energies and disowning the opposite energies — we experience our life as limited and frustrating. We become stuck in old roles and patterns. This is not conducive to an experience of prosperity.

The more we learn to accept and express all aspects of who we are, the more freedom, satisfaction, and wholeness we experience, and the more prosperous we feel. Also, since money is a mirror of our consciousness, the more balanced and integrated we become, the more likely it is that our financial affairs will reflect that by flowing in a balanced, trouble-free way.

I have found the work of Drs. Hal and Sidra Stone* to be particularly effective in teaching us how to integrate the many diverse energies of life. The Stones are psychotherapists who have developed a map of the psyche called the Psychology of Selves, and have created the powerful technique of Voice Dialogue. I am using some of their concepts and terminology in the following sections.

Steps Toward Balance

Step One

The first thing we need to do is recognize that we each contain all the different energies of the universe. They live within us as different "selves" or "subpersonalities" within our personality structure. Some of these subpersonalities are already highly developed and form the major part of our conscious personality. These are called our "primary selves." We all have a number of primary selves who generally work together to help us survive and succeed in life. For example, a few of my primary selves are the super-responsible one, the pusher, the pleaser, the caretaker, the teacher/healer. We usually develop our primary selves fairly early in life and they generally remain an active part of our personality throughout our lives. They more or less run our lives, making most of our choices and decisions according to what they feel is important.

*You will find the Stones' books and tapes listed in the Recommended Resources section.

There are many other energies, or selves, within us that are relatively undeveloped. These are called "disowned selves." Some of these selves may be repressed or held down by the primary selves for fear that they will be harmful or will incur judgment or criticism. For example, my caretaking primary self used to block the energy in me that would put my own needs first, because it feared I would be perceived as selfish.

Our disowned selves form the unconscious part of our personality. We may not know about them at all, or we may try to hide them from the world or even from ourselves by denying them. However, the disowned selves are important parts of us. Not only can we not get rid of them, we actually need the qualities they hold in order to make our lives more balanced, richer, and fuller. So life has a way of putting us into situations where we are forced to confront, acknowledge, and develop our disowned selves.

Our primary selves are usually uncomfortable with our disowned selves and try to keep them from being expressed. The primary selves fear that if these opposite energies come forth, they will take over and control our lives. However, even the primary selves eventually realize that we need some balance. Once the primary selves are reassured that we are searching for balance, and not going to an opposite extreme, they usually become willing to cooperate in the process.

Step Two

We need to recognize our main primary selves. What energies have we developed most strongly? What qualities are we most identified with? The following exercise will help you begin to identify your primary selves.

PRIMARY SELVES EXERCISE #1

Imagine describing yourself as objectively as possible to someone. What words would you use to describe yourself? Write a list of your main personality characteristics in the space below. Concentrate mainly on describing yourself as you normally operate in the world. You might imagine how someone who knows you fairly well, but not intimately — perhaps a casual friend or coworker — might describe you. Try not to judge these qualities as good or bad, just describe objectively how you behave a majority of the time.

Here are examples of three different people's lists:

KAREN	IAN	GEORGE
Outgoing	Musical	Ambitious
Friendly	Quiet	Self-confident
Energetic	Artistic	Powerful
Rebellious	Shy	Focused
Independent	Vegetarian	Active
Strong	Humorous	Hardworking
Disorganized	Spontaneous	Responsible
Talkative	Intuitive	Perfectionist
Enthusiastic	Spiritual	Detail-oriented
Athletic		Judgmental

When you have completed this step, you will have a pretty good list of some of your main primary selves.

LIST OF PRIMARY QUALITIES

Step Three

Acknowledge and appreciate those primary selves. Here are some exercises to help you get to know and appreciate your primary selves.

PRIMARY SELVES EXERCISE #2

Think and write about when, why, and how you developed each of your primary selves. Were some of them modeled after one of your parents, or another early role model or influence? Were any of them developed in an effort to be different from a parent or sibling? Are some of your primary selves the disowned selves of the rest of your family?

How did it help or serve you to develop the particular primary selves that you did? How have your primary selves helped you to survive or succeed in life? How have they protected you and attempted to take care of you?

Primary Selves Exercise #3

Once you've explored these questions and have some sense of how your primary selves have served you, try this exercise:

Close your eyes and imagine one of your primary selves as if it were an actual person. You might see a mental picture of it — how it's dressed, what it's doing — or you might just get a feeling of it. For example, I imagine my responsible self as a strong woman, slightly stooped from carrying the weight of the world on her shoulders, and feeling really tired.

In your mind, imagine thanking that part of you for all that it has done for you. Really let it know that you appreciate the job it has done and is doing for you, and the important role it plays in your life. Let it know that even though you need more balance in your life, and are going to explore some other energies, you never want to lose the qualities this part brings you. You still want it to do its job, but hopefully, that job will become a little easier as you become more balanced.

Now repeat this exercise with each primary self. This may be far too much to do at one time; if so, do it over a period of time.

Step Four

Once you begin to become aware of your primary selves, you are no longer 100 percent identified with them. You begin to develop a little separation from them. You recognize that they are not who you are, they are only parts of who you are. Who you are is much bigger and has the ability to contain and express all the energies.

This experience of separating from our primary selves is the most important step in consciousness growth. The part of us that is able to *recognize* the primary selves, instead of *identifying* with them, is called the "aware ego." The job of the aware ego is to keep gaining more consciousness about all our different aspects, without being identified with any of them. Once we have begun to develop an aware ego, we have some conscious choice about which part of us we want to express at any given time. The development of an aware ego is a gradual, life-long process, but every step we take makes a difference.

Step Five

Identify some of the disowned selves you need or want to develop. You can start by thinking of polarities.

POLARITY EXERCISE

To find out what your disowned selves are, take a look at your list of primary selves and think of an opposite for each one. If the words you come up with for the opposites are very negative, see if you can think of the positive essence underneath your negative judgment. Try to think of the value, benefit, or balance this energy might bring you. For example, if one of your primary selves is responsible, and the opposite of this is irresponsible, the positive essence of irresponsible could be carefree. If you have a very caring, giving primary self, you might think the opposite of that is selfish, which sounds negative. The positive essence of selfish could be "self-loving" or "caring for self."

Write the positive word next to its more negative form as shown on the following page.

For example:

Primary Qualities	Opposite Qualities	Positive Essence
Hardworking	Lazy	Relaxed
Strong	Weak	Vulnerable
Responsible	Irresponsible	Carefree
Caretaking	Selfish	Caring for self
Intelligent	Stupid	Innocent
Accepting	Judgmental	Discerning

LIST YOUR QUALITIES

Primary Qualities	Opposite Qualities	Positive Essence

List Your Qualities

Primary Qualities	Opposite Qualities	Positive Essence

If you can't think of an opposite quality for any of your primary qualities, or you can't think of a positive aspect for one of those opposite qualities, that's okay. Just leave it for now, and see if anything comes to you later.

Remember that we are talking here about balance. The idea is not to get rid of anything or throw anything out, but rather to find the appropriate balance of energies that can help you live your life in a more satisfying manner.

Can you see how any of these opposite qualities might actually be something that you need in order to bring more balance into your life? Is so, write about it here:

Step Six

Think of some ways you can take small, gradual steps in the direction of developing a disowned self, while still keeping your primary strengths.

If you are identified with giving, you might start to develop your receiving side, first by just practicing breathing in deeply, letting yourself receive the life force fully. Then, the next time someone pays you a compliment or expresses appreciation, let yourself breathe in deeply and really receive the acknowledgment. After that, you might practice asking for something you need or want — a hug, a listening ear, some help with a project, a small gift. Take your time with this; it is a gradual process.

If you have disowned some aspects of your creativity, think of steps you can take to get in touch with that part of yourself and begin letting it out. Start with fairly nonthreatening things — reading books on the subject, writing about it in a journal, or doing a small creative project. Then proceed with something a little riskier, like taking lessons or a class, or doing a somewhat larger creative project. Do it for your own enjoyment and try not to worry too much about what others think.

The key here is this: We must learn to honor all the energies of life. When confronted with a set of polarities (within ourselves or externally), we must recognize that there is truth and value in both sides, and embrace it all.

Once we can make friends with all aspects of ourselves, we have access to our full repertoire of energies. This allows us to deal with the various challenges and experiences of life much more creatively and appropriately than when we are stuck in rigid roles. This also contributes greatly to our sense of prosperity.

The following exercises will help you to take steps to separate a bit more from identifying with your primary selves, start to develop your aware ego, and begin to create some space for your disowned energies to come forth and become part of your life.

Exploring Polarities Exercise

Let's work with a few polarities.

To begin, we need to acknowledge how we see ourselves. After reading the description of each set of polarities, rate yourself on a scale of one to ten regarding each of the qualities below, ten being most true of you. You may find that you are very developed on one side of each polarity, and undeveloped on the other. This would likely indicate that one is a primary self for you, and the other is a disowned self. If so, you might think of some ways to begin exploring and expressing the less developed side.

In some cases, you might find that you score yourself high on *both* sides of the polarity. That would indicate that you already have a good balance of both qualities. If you score yourself low on both sides, you may work on developing *both* aspects.

Active and Receptive

One very important and primary pair of contrasting energies within us consists of the active and receptive, or dynamic and magnetic aspects. I often refer to these as the fundamental masculine and feminine principles of the universe.

Every one of us, whether man or woman, has both of these aspects within us. We need to develop both of these energies and allow them to work together rather than be in conflict with each other.

There are two basic ways to have power or get what you want in life: The active (masculine) mode is to go after it and get it, to make it happen. The receptive (feminine) mode is to attract it, magnetize it, to allow it to happen.

The active mode requires focus, aggressiveness, confidence, the ability to do, the ability to persist, and the willingness to risk. The receptive mode requires openness,

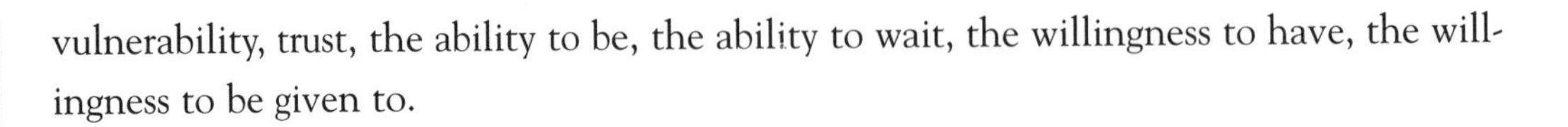

vulnerability, trust, the ability to be, the ability to wait, the willingness to have, the willingness to be given to.

This is me:

1	2	3	4	5	6	7	8	9	10	ACTIVE
1	2	3	4	5	6	7	8	9	10	RECEPTIVE

Write about anything you observe about your relationship with these two polarities:

If you are more strongly developed on one side than the other, what steps could you take to develop greater balance?

Giving and Receiving

Our abilities to give and to receive are at the core of our capacity to create and experience true prosperity.

We each receive certain gifts when we come into this life, in the form of our special talents, interests, and attributes, as well as our universal human characteristics such as our ability to love and care for one another.

When we do our best to live our truth and express ourselves as authentically as possible, sharing ourselves as we are genuinely moved to, we naturally give our gifts to others and to the world.

In return, we may receive acknowledgment, appreciation, validation, nurturing, love, and, in certain circumstances, money or other material rewards. Receiving in these ways allows us to replenish the life force that we have "spent," which in turn enables us to continue giving.

So receiving and giving are opposite energies that are inextricably linked together in the natural flow of life, like inhaling and exhaling. If one aspect of that cycle doesn't function, the entire cycle ceases to function and the life force cannot move freely. If you can't inhale, you will soon have nothing to exhale, and before long, your body will be unable to continue living.

Rate yourself on a scale of one to ten regarding each of the qualities below, ten being most true of you.

This is me:

1 2 3 4 5 6 7 8 9 10 GIVING
1 2 3 4 5 6 7 8 9 10 RECEIVING

Here is an exercise for those who score higher in giving than receiving:

Stand with your feet shoulder-width apart. Reach your arms up and out, so your upper body forms a Y; palms up and open.

While your hands are in the air, look up slightly, as if a thread ran from your chest to a cloud directly above you. Breathe deeply. Your back may crack gently as you stretch your arms.

Release all fears and worries. Imagine you are being given everything you need to feel prosperous — love, money, respect, joy — everything you desire. Imagine you are receiving acknowledgment, payment, and support from all directions.

When you feel complete, say thank you. Bring your arms down slowly. Let your hands hang at your side for a moment or two while you breathe deeply.

This is a good thing to do several times a day just in terms of stretching your body.

Here is an exercise for those who score higher in receiving than giving:

Give whatever you can responsibly spare from this week's expenses. Put it in an envelope and send it off with a note to a local charity; it is a gift you wanted to make to them. Doing it anonymously might feel even more appropriate to you.

Doing and Being

Doing and being are another important pair of opposite energies that are closely related to the ones we've been discussing. Doing is a state of focused, directed, goal-oriented activity. It enables us to handle the business of life and accomplish all the things that we need and want to do. Pure being is a state where we can fully experience the present moment, without thought of the past or future. It allows us to drop into a deeper place where we can connect with our spiritual nature. Doing is primarily the realm of the personality, while being takes us into the realm of the soul.

These energies are equally important. Without the ability to do, we would be helpless and frustrated. Without the ability to be we would feel empty and our lives would seem meaningless. Most of us are more comfortable and developed in one mode or the other. The more we can bring these energies into balance in our lives, the greater our experience of prosperity.

This is me:

1 2 3 4 5 6 7 8 9 10 DOING
1 2 3 4 5 6 7 8 9 10 BEING

Here is an exercise for those who identify more with doing. Find a beautiful, peaceful secluded spot somewhere outdoors. Sit or lie down in a comfortable place. Spend at least fifteen minutes (preferably twenty or thirty minutes) quietly observing this place. Are there any animals, birds, or insects here? What are they doing? Notice the trees, plants, rocks, clouds, breezes. See if you can sit here until you feel quiet and peaceful.

Here is an exercise for those who identify more with being.

Think of something that you've wanted to do or considered doing, but for one reason or another haven't gotten around to. Go and do it.

Other Polarities

Do this same exercise with a few more polarities. Write a little about how you experience these polarities in your life, and steps you could take toward greater balance.

Responsible and Carefree

This is me:

1	2	3	4	5	6	7	8	9	10	RESPONSIBLE
1	2	3	4	5	6	7	8	9	10	CAREFREE

Rational and Intuitive

This is me:

1	2	3	4	5	6	7	8	9	10	RATIONAL
1	2	3	4	5	6	7	8	9	10	INTUITIVE

Caretaking Others and Self-Caring

This is me:

1	2	3	4	5	6	7	8	9	10	CARETAKING OTHERS
1	2	3	4	5	6	7	8	9	10	SELF-CARING

Structure and Flow

Flow is the natural, spontaneous movement of energy. Structure is the principle that creates order and boundaries. Like every other set of polarities, they are both very important and we need to find an appropriate balance of these energies in order to experience prosperity.

Once again, many of us are more developed and more comfortable with one of these principles than the other. Those who are more identified with structure like to plan and organize their lives and are generally good at managing details. Those who identify mainly with flow like to follow their energy as spontaneously as possible and tend to focus on the bigger vision and pay less attention to details. Structured people often approach things in a more rational, analytical way, while flowing people rely more on their intuition and feelings.

This is me:

1 2 3 4 5 6 7 8 9 10 STRUCTURE
1 2 3 4 5 6 7 8 9 10 FLOW

STRUCTURE AND FLOW FINANCIAL EXERCISES

If you are strongly identified with flow and not as developed in structure, you probably manage your finances in a loose, spontaneous way, not paying too much attention to details, and "trusting the universe" to take care of things. You may have resisted or skipped doing the exercise in the Awareness section on tracking your money. If so, go back and give it a try. Here are three other exercises that won't sound like much fun to you, but in the long run will be very liberating and empowering:

1. Balance your checkbook every month. If you don't know how, ask a "structured" type of friend or someone at your bank to teach you. You will probably need to close your old account and open a new one in order to start this process. Once you learn, it's easy. Believe it or not, it can be really fun and satisfying, like putting the pieces of a puzzle together.

2. Use the information you get from the Tracking Your Money exercise to create a basic budget for yourself. Most "flow" people are afraid of budgets, seeing them as rigid, authoritarian documents that will deprive them of things they enjoy. A budget is really an accurate picture of what you earn and spend, and should realistically include everything you really want and need. It's a plan you create for yourself to help you get clear on your choices and priorities. For more information and help, refer to either of the books suggested on page 67.

3. Try using this affirmation, "When I manage my money carefully, I feel empowered and prosperous."

If you are strongly identified with structure and flow is more disowned for you, you probably manage your money carefully and sensibly. That's fine, but it may be time to practice loosening up a little. Here are three exercises for you to do:

1. Go out on a shopping trip with the express purpose of spontaneously buying yourself something that you really want but normally wouldn't spend money on because you consider it too frivolous. You can do this appropriately, in proportion to your financial circumstances. If you are on a very tight budget, just spend five or ten dollars on some little thing you want; if you are wealthy, spend whatever you want.

2. Every month send money to a cause that you really believe in but normally don't think you could afford to help. Again, make it an amount appropriate to your situation; just give something that you normally wouldn't give. Or begin tithing a certain percent of your income to an organization that gives you spiritual inspiration.

3. Try using the affirmation, "I trust the universe to always provide whatever I need."

If you are fairly developed in both structure and flow, congratulations! Enjoy your prosperity.

THE COSTANZA EXERCISE

A particularly funny episode of the television show *Seinfeld* featured the character George Costanza feeling so frustrated with the consequences of his decisions that he decided to react, for an entire day, the opposite of how he was inclined to act.

"That's the ticket! I'm going to do the opposite of what I would normally do, in any given circumstance, and my life will improve." And he began to play with reacting, stopping himself, then reacting in a totally different fashion than the norm for him.

Making this minor adjustment on an experimental basis is a form of risk taking for the nonprimary aspects of yourself, your "disowned" selves. Do this once this week, and you can give yourself a gold star for risk taking! This doesn't mean, of course, that you throw yourself into a dangerous situation. But when a situation arises in which you must choose a course of action, stop and consider your choices, and if it feels challenging yet safe, do the opposite of what you're most inclined to do. Do a "Costanza."

I was going to:

But instead I:

It felt:

Identifying Yourself Clearly

Use the diagram below to identify yourself more clearly. We want to see to what degree we identify with these aspects of ourselves. Mark each quality with a number from one to ten, ten being the most like you, the most accurate description of how you see yourself, and one being the least like you.

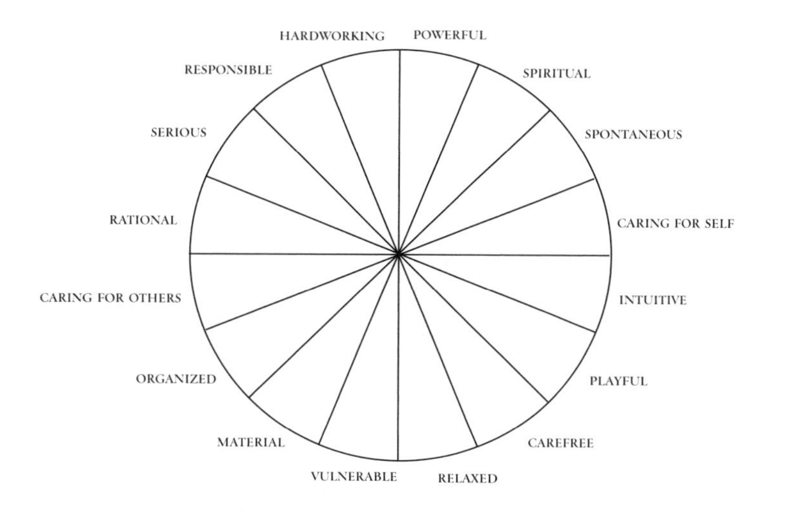

The qualities that score highest most likely describe characteristics of your primary selves. The lowest scores are probably your disowned selves.

Four Selves Exercise

List the two qualities from the wheel that score higher than the others. For example, Janet's two highest scores are Responsible and Hardworking. These are primary selves. List your two highest-scoring qualities:

1) ______________________ 2) ______________________

List the two that score the lowest. These are disowned selves.

For example, Janet's two lowest scores are Playful and Relaxed. List your two lowest-scoring qualities:

1) ______________________ 2) ______________________

Now develop a "character" that best represents each of these four qualities in your imagination. We are going to arrange a fictional meeting for these four selves. Write a brief description of each of your characters on the following page. You might want to use a different colored pen for each one.

My Characters

When you've finished, imagine these four selves seated in a circle. They have come together to decide how to create more prosperity. Record their conversation below verbatim, including any "interruptions," conflicts, or doubts. This is an equal opportunity discussion, so make sure the "disowned" aspects you've discovered get a chance to have their say.

Using the previous example:

Two of Janet's primary selves are the Hardworker and the Responsible Mother. Two of her more disowned energies are the Easygoing Guy and the Playful Child.

Hardworker: *Well, the only way for Janet to get more prosperous is to work harder! She only works forty to fifty hours a week. If she worked more, her boss would be impressed and give her a raise.*

Responsible Mother: *Wait a minute! Money isn't everything. She won't feel prosperous unless she has time to take care of her home, and spends quality time with her children.*

Playful Child: *What about me? I just want to have some fun! I want to go to Disneyland!*

Easygoing Guy: *To me, prosperity would be spending a lot of time relaxing at the beach.*

. . . and so on.

Read over the dialogue you've "recorded." Now imagine that you are the "aware ego" — the one who is aware of all of these selves but not identified with any of them. Your job is to appreciate all of them and let them know that their needs and feelings are important. Are there any compromises that can be made among these selves that would bring them into harmony? Can you think of any small actions you might take to support the aspects of yourself that aren't getting what they need? Make a few notes about the possibilities below:

Reviewing the Steps Toward Balance

A summary of the steps that I have found helpful in effectively balancing our inner polarities follows:

Step One: Recognize that you contain all the different energies of the universe.

Step Two: Recognize what your main primary selves are.

Step Three: Acknowledge and appreciate those primary selves.

Step Four: Experience the separation from your primary selves — become less identified with any one aspect, and begin to develop an aware ego.

Step Five: Identify some of the disowned selves you need or want to develop.

Step Six: Take small, gradual steps in the direction of developing a disowned self, while still keeping the primary strengths that you have.

Energy-Balancing Meditation

Relax in a comfortable place and close your eyes. Think of one of your primary selves. Imagine that you can bring the energy of that self fully into your body. This will probably feel quite familiar, since this is a self that you have been very much identified with. Notice how you feel when the energy of this self "occupies" you. Be aware of how your body feels, what your posture is like, how you are breathing. Notice what perceptions you have from this self, and how you experience life.

Once you have fully experienced this energy, imagine that you can let go of this self for the moment and release its energy from your body. Place it next to you, on the right or left, whichever you intuitively feel is right. It's near you, so you can bring it back in whenever you need or want it.

Now think of an opposite self, one that has been less developed or more disowned for you. See if you can bring the energy of this self into your body and experience it. This may feel much less familiar. Again, notice how your body feels with this energy. It may feel very different than with the first energy. Be aware of how you perceive the world around you, and how you experience life from this energy. Now release this energy from your body, and place it near you on the opposite side of you from the first energy. See if you can feel, sense, or imagine both energies, one on either side of you. When you can be conscious of two opposite energies at the same time, you are experiencing a moment of "aware ego." From this place you have conscious choice; you could choose to bring in either one of these energies, or perhaps a bit of both, depending on what you need at any given moment. This is a very stable, balanced position.

You can repeat this exercise with as many pairs of opposite energies as you wish.

Following Your Truth

If prosperity is an experience of having enough of what we truly need and desire, how do we know what we truly need and desire? We've all had the experience of thinking we need something, or desperately wanting a certain object, experience, or relationship, only to find: (1) Once we got what we wanted, it didn't make us happy or fulfill us in the way we had hoped, or (2) We didn't get it and life worked out okay anyway.

On an emotional level, we've all experienced not getting our needs met or not having our desires fulfilled in life. As a result, we've all suffered some degree of disappointment, frustration, and pain. If the pain has been great, we may have decided, consciously or unconsciously, to protect ourselves from further disappointment by denying our need and giving up our dreams and desires. Unfortunately, when we shut down in this way, we block the life force from moving through us; we become depressed and numb.

So how do we relate to our needs and desires in a healthy way that can bring us true prosperity?

First, let's reflect on the difference between a need and a desire. As I see it, a need is something essential for our survival and basic satisfaction. We have needs on all levels —

physical, mental, emotional, and spiritual. Our true desires are our yearning for the things that we feel will enhance and enrich our lives and our development. These are not two separate and sharply defined categories. Rather, our needs and desires exist on a spectrum, something like this:

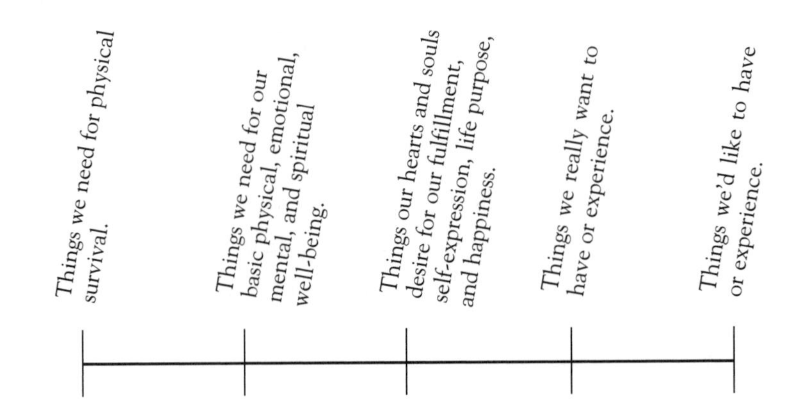

Obviously, if our basic survival needs are not met, nothing else is going to matter for long. In general, the further we move along the spectrum, fulfilling each category, the greater our experience of prosperity.

False Cravings

There is another type of desire, which I call a false craving, or addiction. A false craving is the desire for something that we think we want, but when we get it, it doesn't really satisfy us or enhance our life. We are lured by false cravings when we are not conscious of our true needs and desires, or don't know how to go about fulfilling them.

When we continue to pursue a false craving to the point where it becomes obsessive and out of control, it becomes an addiction. An addiction appears to satisfy some of our needs momentarily, but not for long, because it does not address our real needs.

One of the most damaging things about addiction is that it very effectively keeps us from getting in touch with and learning to satisfy our true needs and desires. For that reason, and many others, if we hope to create true prosperity in our lives, we must first acknowledge and begin to heal any addictive patterns we may have. And most of us do have them, to one degree or another.

In this day and age, most of us are aware of a virtual epidemic of drug and alcohol addiction in our society. Also, we are becoming aware of how many of us suffer from food addictions or eating disorders such as anorexia and bulimia. Other forms of common addictive behavior include sexual addictions, various forms of obsession about relationships, and workaholism. Even meditation can become an addiction for some. Anything we do habitually to avoid the pain of not having our real needs met can be an addiction.

There are many forms of addictive behavior related to money. The addiction to gambling is extremely common. Many people have a shopping or spending addiction; we may joke about it, but it can be serious if it's used habitually to avoid addressing our real needs and feelings. The obsession to earn more and more money even when one already has considerable wealth is surely an addiction, an attempt to satisfy a craving for security, power, or status that somehow is never enough. In their book, *The Money Drunk: 90 Days to Financial Freedom*, Mark Bryan and Julia Cameron describe five types of money addicts: the compulsive spender, the big deal chaser, the maintenance money drunk, the poverty addict, and the cash co-dependent. Money-related addictions may give us a temporary illusion of prosperity, but they are guaranteed to sabotage any possibility of enjoying true financial prosperity.

Basically, our addictions are the ways that we unconsciously try to fill the emptiness that we feel inside. This emptiness can only be filled by the things that we truly need, such as a deep connection to our spiritual source, a close relationship with the natural world, a strong sense of self, and loving contact with other humans. In order to fill those needs, we must first allow ourselves to feel them.

An addiction is not something to be ashamed of (although most of us are). We all have them in one form or another. The great thing is this: When our addictive behavior becomes painful and self-defeating enough, it forces us to begin or deepen our healing process.

We are fortunate enough to live in a time when many resources exist to help and support us in this process. Twelve-step programs such as Alcoholics Anonymous, Al-Anon, Overeaters Anonymous, Gamblers Anonymous, Debtors Anonymous, and so forth seem to be the most effective way for most people to deal with an addictive process. There are also many therapists and support groups that specialize in these issues. If you think you might have an addiction problem, I urge you to reach out for the appropriate help. It could be the most important step toward health, happiness, and true prosperity you ever take!

False Craving Exercise

Ask yourself these questions and write the answers.

What do I tend to do when I feel a need and I don't really know what it is, or when I want to avoid my feelings?

What could I do instead that would truly nurture and support me, help me get in touch with my real feelings, and meet my real needs?

Is there a recent time when I used a substance such as food, sugar, alcohol, or another drug to soothe myself, or bought something I didn't need to "cheer myself up"? What did I really need and how could I have taken care of myself more appropriately?

Discovering Our True Desires

Once we have begun the healing process with our false cravings and addictions, we can begin to discover our true needs and desires and learn how to go about fulfilling them.

Our true desires come from our hearts and souls, and we need to honor and trust them. Life guides us in the direction we need to go, through our deep longing. Our desires motivate us to move along our path, learning, growing, and developing our unique form of creative expression. Our dreams guide us to the fulfillment of our life purpose.

Getting in Touch with Your Needs and Desires

Here is an exercise to help you get in touch with your needs and desires.

1) Find a quiet place where you will be undisturbed for an hour or two, in a comfortable, nurturing environment. Bring a notebook and pen. Take some time to think deeply about what you truly want in your life, what is most important to you. What do you need on each of these levels: spiritually, mentally, emotionally, and physically?

2) Write down everything that comes to your mind. Include tangible and intangible things. Remember that some of our needs change at different times in our lives. Include whatever is important to you now.

3) Then look at each item, and write about why it is important to you. See if you can break everything down to its essential components.

Example:

I want a beautiful home.

Why?

So I can be safe and comfortable, and live in a beautiful environment. I want to express my creative energy through furnishing and decorating it, and create a nest in which to raise my children. Also, I want others to respect the fact that I've earned enough money to buy such a nice house.

Can you identify the needs behind this?

The important elements for me in this desire are safety, comfort, creative self-expression, nurturing my family, and recognition from others for my ability to effectively manifest my power in the world.

As you can see, there are a number of important emotional and creative needs wrapped up in the desire for a seemingly external thing.

Remember that the process of creating prosperity rests on knowing what your needs and desires really are. Recognizing and consciously taking responsibility for your own needs is an essential and powerful step toward creating what you want.

MY NEEDS AND DESIRES

Trusting Intuition

The best way I have found to follow my true desires is to pay attention to my intuitive sense. We all have within us a deep sense of what we need, and what is right and true for us. To access this we need to pay attention to our feelings and our intuition. Our higher power speaks to us through our intuition. Your intuition is the "gut" feeling within you — the source of your deepest personal truth. We need to learn to listen deeply to ourselves and to trust what we hear. And we need to risk acting on what we feel to be true. Even if we make mistakes, we must do this in order to learn and grow.

How do we get in touch with our intuition? There is no single answer to that question. The process is different for everyone. Some people listen for their intuitive guidance through meditation; others listen through art, dance, sports, music, writing, walks through nature, or moments of stillness. Your intuition may actually come to you as an inner voice, or you may be guided by a strong feeling or hunch, an image, or an inner sound or vibration.

As discussed in the Awareness and Healing and Growth sections of the workbook, we have many different "voices" inside of us, so it does take some practice for most of us to learn to distinguish our intuitive guidance from some of the others. It does have a particular feeling or vibration about it that we can learn to recognize.

Our inner guidance is always within us, but we aren't always able to access it. If we are caught up in our rational mind, we may have difficulty connecting with our intuition; we may need to learn to relax and let go. If we are emotionally blocked or upset, we may need some emotional healing or nurturing before we can access intuition. It's a gradual process, and a very rewarding one.*

---

*I have written extensively on this topic in *Living in the Light* and other books, and I have several tapes with guided meditations on developing intuition and inner guidance. See Recommended Resources.

The following exercises will guide you in contacting your intuition, help you practice paying attention to your inner wisdom, and teach you how to recognize it clearly. The exercises also may help you realize that you're already in contact with your intuition.

Contacting and Recognizing Your Intuition

Sit or lie down in a comfortable position in a quiet place. Close your eyes and relax. Take several slow, deep breaths, relaxing your body more with each breath. Relax your mind and let your thoughts drift, but don't hold onto any thought. Imagine that your mind becomes as quiet as a peaceful lake.

Now focus your conscious awareness into a deep place in your body, in the area of your stomach or solar plexus. It should be the place in your body where you feel your "gut feelings" reside. This is the physical place where you can most easily contact you intuition.

Imagine that you have a wise being living inside there. You might have an image of what this wise being looks like, or you might just sense that it is there. This wise being is really a part of you — your intuitive self. You can communicate with it by talking to it silently. Ask a question, such as, "What do I need to be aware of right now?" or make a request, such as, "Please bring me clarity about my direction." Then relax, don't think too hard, sit quietly and be open to whatever feeling, thought, or image may come to you in response. Just sit for awhile and "be with" whatever comes, even if you don't understand it. The responses are usually very simple; they relate to the present moment (not the past or future), and they "feel right." If you don't receive an immediate response, let go and go about your life. The answer will come later, either from inside of you in the form of a feeling or idea, or from outside through a person, a book, an event, or in some other way.

For example, you might say, "Intuition, tell me what I need to know about ___________ [a particular issue in your life]. What do I need to do in this situation?"

If something comes to you that feels right, trust it and see if you can take a step toward acting on it. If it is truly your intuition, you will find that it leads to a feeling of greater aliveness and power, and more opportunities begin to open up for you. If it doesn't seem right, you may not have been truly acting from your intuition but from a different voice in you. Go back and ask for clarification.

Do this simple meditation as often as you can. It's great to do first thing in the morning or last thing at night.

It takes practice to hear and trust your intuition. The more you do it, the easier it will become. Eventually you will be able to contact your intuition, ask yourself questions, and know that in the "wise being" within you, an incredible source of power and strength is available to answer your questions and guide you. As you grow more sensitive to this guidance from the intuitive feelings within, you will gain a sense of knowing what you need to do in any situation. Your intuitive power is always available to guide you whenever you need it. It will open to you as soon as you are willing to trust yourself and your inner knowledge.

Nondominant Hand Writing Exercise

Another good way to practice getting in touch with your intuition is through nondominant hand writing.

If you are right-handed, let your right hand represent your conscious, rational mind, and your left hand represent your intuitive mind. (If you are left-handed, reverse it.) Use a different colored pen for each hand.

Write a simple question that is of importance to you with your dominate hand. Then without thinking too much, begin to answer it with your other hand. This may feel difficult. (You'll feel like you're in kindergarten again!) Do it anyway. Continue the dialogue as long as it feels appropriate. You may be surprised at what you learn.

Example:

Right hand: *What direction should I take my work?*

Left hand: *Relax, don't think so much. You are not trusting what you already know. You don't need to take a direction, you already have and the doors will open when you begin to trust yourself. Everything will work out fine.*

Releasing and Receiving Meditation

Sit or lie down in a comfortable position. Close your eyes and breathe slowly, gently, and deeply for a few minutes, relaxing your body and mind. Keep bringing your attention back to your breath, feeling the air as it moves in and out of your lungs, and imagining it bringing energy to every cell in your body.

Each time you exhale, imagine that you are releasing whatever you no longer need — old beliefs, old patterns, old cravings or addictive behaviors. You are not trying to get rid of anything, you are gently and naturally releasing anything that is ready to go. This is happening on a cellular level.

Each time you inhale, you are breathing in life energy, receiving from it exactly what you truly need and want right now. Every cell of your body is being nurtured by the life force.

Now imagine yourself going through life, deeply attuned to your inner intuitive guidance. You have the courage to live your truth, and as a result, you feel yourself moving with the flow of life.

Creating a Vision

To experience prosperous lives, it's important to begin imagining how we would like things to be. Our imagination is a powerful creative tool. Once we can vividly imagine something, we seem to open the doors to manifesting it. As we develop our sense of prosperity, we begin to feel that the universe is abundant, that life is actually trying to bring us what our hearts and souls truly desire — spiritually, mentally, emotionally, as well as physically.

VISUALIZING

Creative visualization is the technique of using your imagination to create what you want in your life. There is nothing at all new, strange, or unusual about creative visualization. You are already using it every day, every minute, in fact. It is your natural power of imagination, the basic creative energy of the universe, that you use constantly, whether or not you are aware of it.

Many of us use creative visualization in a relatively unconscious way. Because of our own deep-seated negative concepts about life, we may have automatically and unconsciously expected and imagined limitation, difficulties, and problems to be our lot in life. To one degree or another, that is what we have created for ourselves.

Learning to use our creative imagination in a more conscious way, as a technique to create what we *truly* want, allows us to tap into the natural goodness and bounty of life.

Don't let the term "visualize" confuse you. It is not at all necessary to mentally see an image. Some people say they see very clear, sharp images when they close their eyes and imagine something. Others don't really "see" anything; they sense or feel it, or they just sort of "think about" it. That's perfectly fine. Some people are more visually oriented than others.

In creating a vision, we use our imagination to create a clear image, idea, or a *feeling sense* of the life we wish to live. If we keep our vision in mind as we go through our process of gaining awareness, healing ourselves, and learning to follow our truth, we are likely to find that in time, our vision begins to manifest itself in our life.

Using Affirmations

Affirmations are one way of supporting and strengthening our vision. To affirm means "to make firm." An affirmation is a strong, positive statement that something is already so. It is a way of "making firm" that which you are imagining.

Most of us are aware of the fact that we have a nearly continuous "dialogue" going on in our minds. The mind is busy "talking" to itself, keeping up an endless commentary about life, the world, our feelings, our problems, and other people.

The words and ideas that run through our minds are very important. Most of the time we aren't consciously aware of this stream of thoughts, and yet what we are "telling ourselves" in our minds is the basis on which we form our experience of reality. Our mental commentary influences and colors our feelings and perceptions about what's going on in our lives, and it is these thought forms that ultimately attract and create everything that happens to us.

Any of us who have practiced meditation knows how difficult it can be to quiet this inner "mind talk," in order to connect with our deeper, wiser intuitive mind; but simply observing our inner dialogue as objectively as possible can help us create affirmations that are particularly effective for us.

For example, I might discover the following statements when observing my thoughts: "I sure wish I could write a book, but I doubt that I can," or "I'm trying to write a book." A helpful affirmation in this case might be, "I am now writing a book" or "I have successfully written a book."

The practice of using affirmations allows us to begin replacing some of our stale or negative mind chatter with more positive ideas and concepts.

Affirmations can be done silently, spoken aloud, written down, or even sung or chanted. Even two minutes a day of repeating effective affirmations can counterbalance years of old mental habits.

Here are some important things to remember about affirmations:

1. Always phrase affirmations in the present tense, not in the future. It's important to create your desire as if it already exists. Don't say, "I will get a wonderful new job," but rather, "I now have a wonderful new job." This is not lying to yourself; it is acknowledging the fact that everything is created first on the inner plane, before it can manifest in external reality.

2. Always phrase affirmations in the most positive way you can. Affirm what you *do* want, not what you *don't* want. Don't say, "I no longer oversleep in the morning," but

rather, "I now wake up on time and full of energy in the morning." This ensures that you are creating the most positive possible mental image.

3. In general, the shorter and simpler the affirmation, the more effective. Affirmations that are long, wordy, and theoretical lose their emotional impact.

4. Always choose affirmations that feel totally right for you. What works for one person may not work at all for another. Of course, you may feel emotional resistance to any affirmation when you first use it, especially one that is really powerful for you and is going to make a real change in your consciousness. That resistance is simply our natural fear of change and growth.

5. Always remember that you are creating something new and fresh. You are not trying to redo or change what already exists. To do so would be to resist what is, which creates conflict and struggle. Take the attitude that you are accepting and handling whatever already exists in your life, and at the same time taking every moment as a new opportunity to begin creating exactly what you desire and will make you feel most prosperous.

6. Affirmations are not meant to contradict or change your feelings or emotions. It is important to accept and experience *all* your feelings, including so-called "negative" ones, without attempting to change them. At the same time, affirmations can help you create a new point of view about life that will enable you to have more and more satisfying experiences from now.

7. Try as much as possible to create a feeling of belief, an experience that your affirmations can be true. Temporarily (at least for a few minutes) suspend your doubts and hesitations, and put your full mental and emotional energy into them.

For many people, affirmations are most powerful and inspiring when they include references to a spiritual source. Mention of God, the Goddess, the Universe, a higher power, spirit, the Earth Mother, divine love, or whatever phrase you prefer adds spiritual energy to your affirmation and acknowledges the universal source of all things.*

Affirmation Exercise

Let's begin to create a vision of prosperity by creating affirmations for a few of our desires. Think of a few desires that you believe will enhance your state of prosperity. List the item or idea on the left; then write a related affirmation on the right.

You may want to add to this list after you have done the Ideal Scene and Ideal Day exercises that follow. Often some hidden desires reveal themselves in those processes.

For example:

Desire	Affirmation
To live in a sunny house.	*I live in sun-drenched house on a hill.*
To learn to play the piano.	*I am learning to play the piano beautifully.*
To find a better job.	*I now have a job I love.*

*This material on visualizing and affirmations was taken from my book *Creative Visualization*. For more information on these techniques, I suggest reading the book.

DESIRE	AFFIRMATION

Desire	Affirmation

Ideal Scene

The process of describing your ideal scene can help you get clearer about what you really want. Imagine you are presently living a truly prosperous life and describe the situation in as much detail as possible. Describe your scene in the present tense, as if it already exists.

If it's helpful, answer each of the following questions as you write:

Where and how are you living?
How do you feel about yourself?
How does your body feel?
How and where do you find your spiritual connection?
What are your relationships like?
How much time do you spend in relationship, and how much time alone?
What kind of work do you do?
How do you express yourself creatively?
What other aspects of your lifestyle can you imagine?
Do you have a sense of community in your life?
In what ways do you make a contribution to others and/or the world?

My Ideal Scene

My Ideal Scene

Keep your ideal scene in your workbook, make copies and put one in your desk or near your bed, or hang it on your wall. Read it often, and make appropriate changes when necessary.

Ideal Day

Now, let's repeat the previous process while focusing on one particular ideal day. Include anything you can imagine, but try to be realistic when it comes to the time frame.

Write down everything you can think of that might be included in your ideal day and describe it in as much detail as possible. Be sure to include how you feel at the end of the day.

Imagine you are just waking up. Describe how you feel and how your ideal day transpires:

My Ideal Day

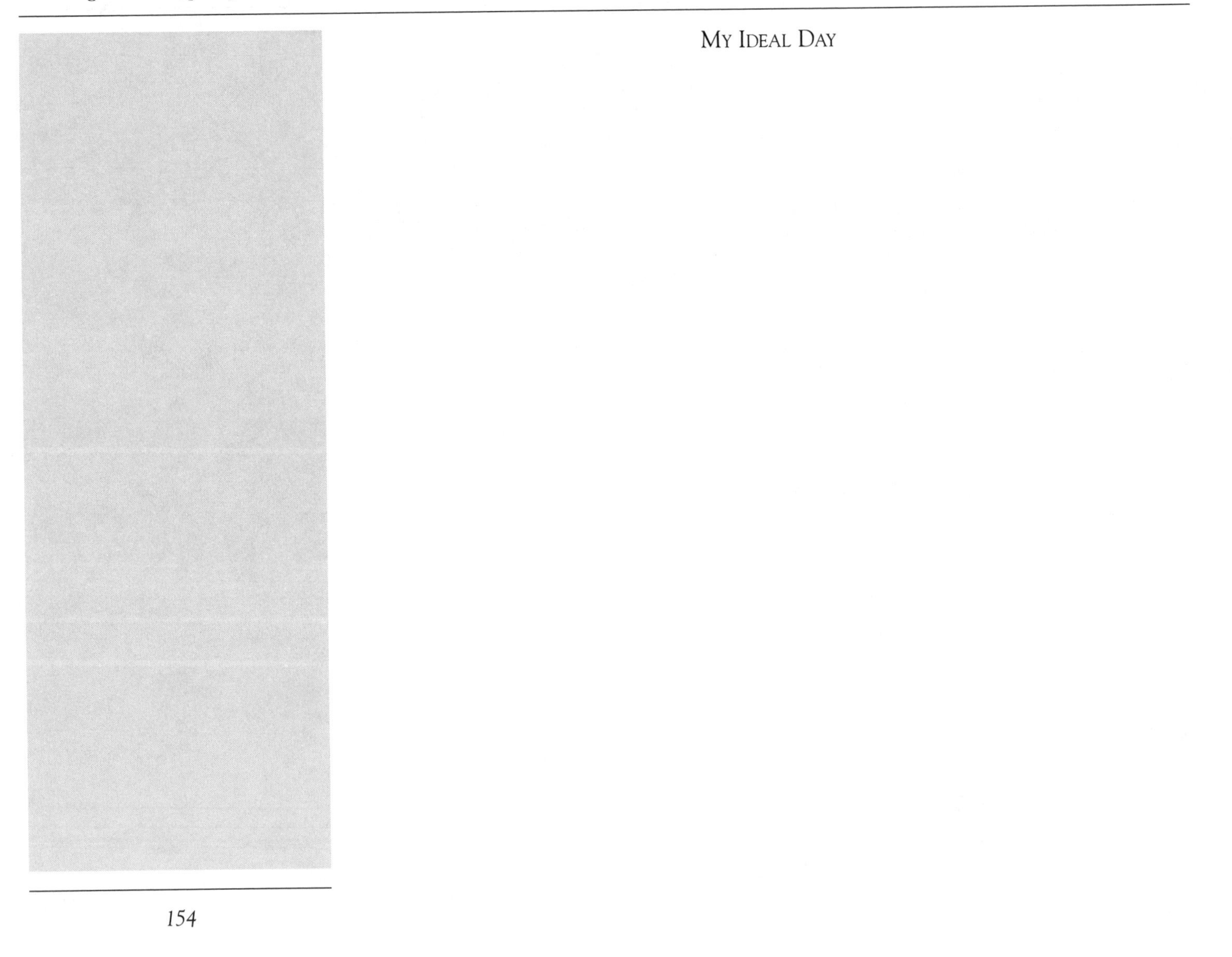

My Ideal Day

My Ideal Day

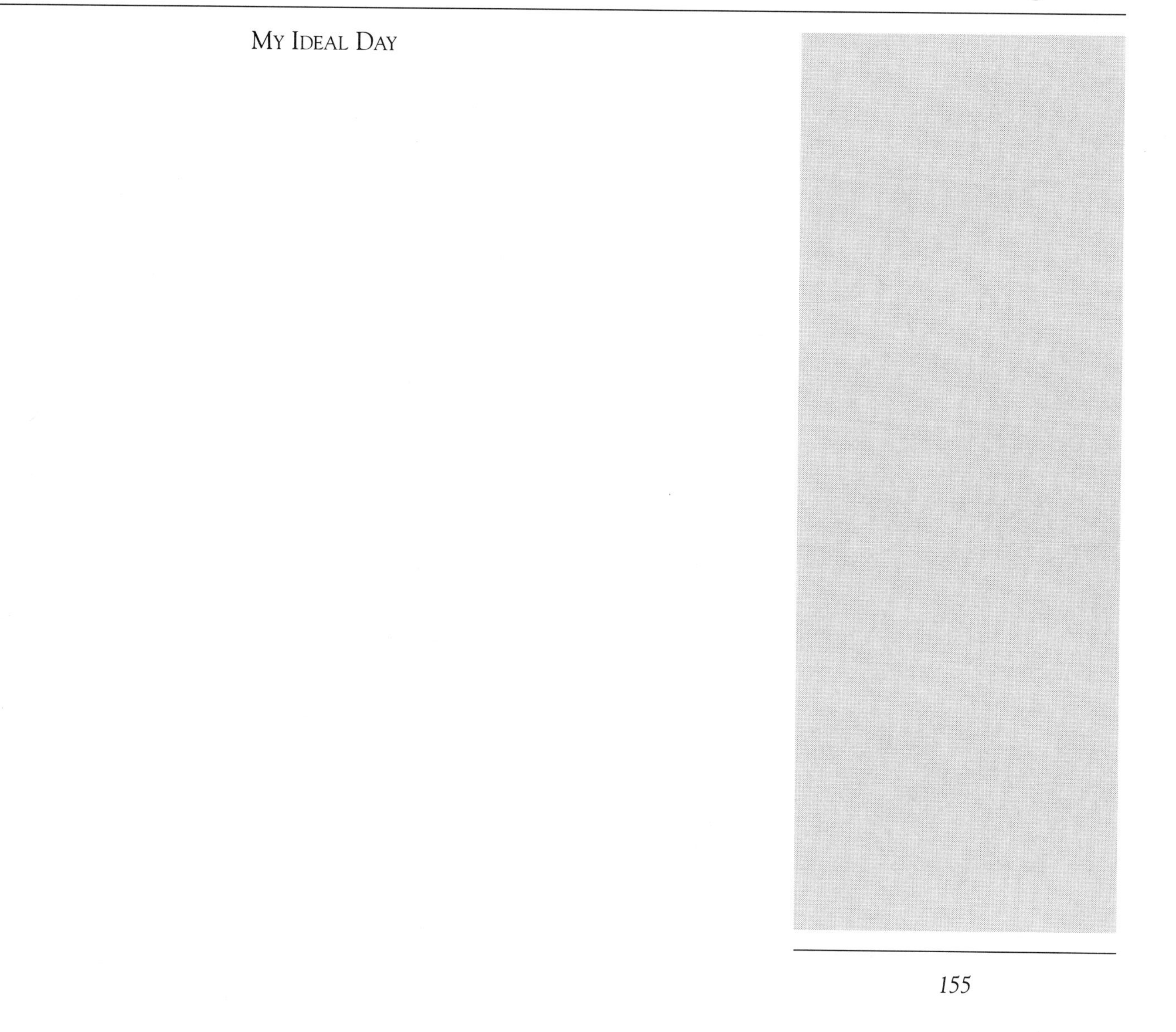

Ideal Scene Meditation

Now that you have a good idea of what elements will give you a greater experience of prosperity, try the following creative visualization exercise, if you wish.

Get in a comfortable position, either sitting or lying down, in a quiet place where you won't be disturbed. Relax your body completely. Starting from your toes and moving up to your scalp, think of relaxing each muscle in your body in turn, letting all tension flow out of your body. Breathe deeply and slowly, from your belly. Count down slowly from ten to one, feeling yourself getting more deeply relaxed with each count.

When you feel deeply relaxed, start to imagine your ideal scene. Imagine yourself there and everything happening just as you want it to. You may imagine what people are saying, or any details that make it more real to you.

You may take a relatively short time or quite a few minutes to do this — whatever feels best to you. Have fun with it. It should be a thoroughly enjoyable experience, like a child daydreaming about what he wants for his birthday.

Now, keeping the idea or image still in your mind, mentally make some very positive affirmation statements to yourself about it (aloud or silently, as you prefer). You can use the affirmations that you created at the beginning of this section or new ones that you develop in the process of writing your ideal scene and ideal day.

Treasure Map

Another wonderful action step you can take toward creating your vision can be done by drawing or painting a picture of your ideal scene, called a "treasure map." Making a treasure map is a very powerful technique, and fun to do.

A treasure map is an actual, physical picture of your desired reality. It is valuable because it forms an especially clear, sharp image that can then attract and focus energy into your goal. It works along the same lines as a blueprint for a building.

You can make a treasure map by drawing or painting it, or by making a collage using pictures and words cut from magazines, books or cards, photographs, lettering, drawings, elements from nature, or anything else that evokes a feeling of prosperity in you. Don't worry if you're not artistically accomplished. Simple, childlike treasure maps are just as effective as great works of art!

Essentially, the treasure map should show you in your ideal scene, with your goal fully realized.

You can create your treasure map on the following page, or on a separate piece of paper or cardboard, so that you can hang it somewhere where you will look at it often.

My Treasure Map

Creating a Vision that Benefits All

None of us exists in a vacuum. We are powerfully affected by the world around us, and we have an equally powerful effect on the world, whether or not we realize it. We are an integral part of the whole. We can only have a truly prosperous life to the extent that our world is prosperous. And our world can only be truly prosperous when we learn to honor and respect the earth we live on, and all the other beings — human and otherwise — who live here as well.

Those of us fortunate enough to live in circumstances where we have the luxury of pursuing personal growth have a responsibility to use what we learn to make the world a healthier, more prosperous place for all.

Since we are all ultimately part of one consciousness, the most effective way to do that is to take responsibility for our own healing. The more conscious and balanced we become, the more we live in integrity and follow our truth, the more healing we bring to the world. We need to ask our inner guidance, too, if there are specific actions we need to take to make our contribution to the world.

On the following page there is beautiful world vision meditation. Should any specific ideas come to you through this meditation, write them down and take the necessary steps available to you to put them into action.

World Vision Meditation

Get comfortable, close your eyes, breathe deeply, and relax. Once again bring to mind your ideal scene for your life. Now expand that to imagine your larger community and the world around you — healed and transformed. Imagine human beings all over the world living in balance and harmony with themselves, one another, and nature. Envision the earth, and all of her children, healthy, flourishing, and truly prosperous.

Setting Goals

Once you have a sense of your overall vision for a truly prosperous life, you can set some specific goals if that feels right to you. There are times in life when it is helpful to set goals, and other times when it is best to let go of goals for a while, and just see where life takes you. If you check in with yourself and it doesn't feel right, skip the goals process for now. If it feels exciting, fun, or helpful, go ahead and go through it.

The following section is set up in two different ways. The first is organized in a time framework. The second is broken into the different areas of life that most affect our experience of prosperity. You can use the first, the second, or both, in either order.

GOALS EXERCISE: SECTION ONE

Take some time to think about your current goals in life — both long and short term. Then write your most important goals for each time frame. Be as expansive as possible on the long-term goals; maintain a more "realistic" point of view with the short-term goals.

Don't worry if you aren't sure exactly what your goals are. Just think of things that feel

right for now; you can always change them later. When writing out your goals, use the present tense, as if they are happening now. This puts each goal in the form of an affirmation. For example: *I am living in a beautiful cottage in the country.*

In ten years, this is how I would like my life to be:

In five years, this is how I would like my life to be:

In one year, this is how I would like my life to be:

My goals for the next month are:

Small steps that I can take now:

If you wish, you can to write your daily and weekly goals on the calendar in the back of the workbook. You can also record the small steps that you have decided to take toward your desires on the calendar. Keep it simple. It's probably best to try no more than three or less goals at a time in the beginning to keep you focused on taking action without overextending yourself.

Goals Exercise: Section Two

We need to invest mentally, emotionally, spiritually, and physically in our visions. Imagining alone is not enough. An equal part of creating our vision is taking action. If you are a person highly identified with the "doing" aspect of yourself, however, you might also want to record nonactions to take! For example, you can use the calendar to remind yourself to stop for a moment and remember how you wanted to feel when you set your goals. The calendar is not just a list of to-do's, as prosperity is not just about doing.

It is sometimes helpful to go through the different areas of our lives that affect our experience of prosperity and get clear on what it is we want and need in each of those areas. Do these at your leisure and change or add to them regularly, if you wish. Our desires do change as we grow.

When you have finished listing your goals, go back through your list. Breathe life into each goal as you read them aloud slowly. After each goal, take another breath, and write down in the space provided below one or more small action steps you can take to move you in the direction of your goal.

You may want to come back to the list daily, to add a new action, to add a reminder, or to check off any action steps you have taken.

For example:

Goal

To live in a sunny cottage in the country.

Action Steps

Post a "wanted" sign at my local market, library, and gym describing the house I'm looking for and the financial range I can afford.

Review the local newspapers for houses to rent/own.

Call the local real estate offices and inform them of my needs.

Personal Growth

Goal

Action Steps

Personal Growth

GOAL

ACTION STEPS

GOAL

ACTION STEPS

GOAL

ACTION STEPS

Body/Health/Appearance

Goal

Action Steps

Goal

Action Steps

Goal

Action Steps

Relationships

Goal

Action Steps

Goal

Action Steps

Goal

Action Steps

Work/Career

GOAL

ACTION STEPS

GOAL

ACTION STEPS

GOAL

ACTION STEPS

Finances

GOAL

ACTION STEPS

GOAL

ACTION STEPS

GOAL

ACTION STEPS

Home/Possessions

GOAL

ACTION STEPS

GOAL

ACTION STEPS

GOAL

ACTION STEPS

Recreation/Travel

GOAL

ACTION STEPS

GOAL

ACTION STEPS

GOAL

ACTION STEPS

Creative Expression/Special Interests

GOAL

ACTION STEPS

GOAL

ACTION STEPS

GOAL

ACTION STEPS

Making a Difference/Service

GOAL

ACTION STEPS

GOAL

ACTION STEPS

GOAL

ACTION STEPS

Once you have created your goals, put them away for a while. Look at them once every few months, or whenever you feel inspired. Change them as needed, and be sure to appreciate your successes, small and great, along the way.

Goals can help us gain clarity, inspiration, and focus. However, they can also work against us if we hold onto them too tightly, or try too hard to make them happen.

Hold your goals lightly, and allow them to change and evolve as you do. You may find that certain things are going as you hoped, while others aren't. You may even find that your whole life is going in a different direction than you expected. Remember that our souls have a purpose in this life that we may not fully understand yet, and everything that happens to us is part of our soul's journey.

Keep learning from whatever comes your way. Continue to follow your intuitive sense. If a certain goal is right for you, it will unfold naturally from this process. Let your inner guidance show you the way. The following page has a meditation that will help you with this process.

Goals Meditation

Sit or lie down in a comfortable position. Close your eyes, relax, and take a few deep, slow breaths. Now imagine that you can travel one year into the future. All of your most important one-year goals have been achieved. You might have a visual image of what this would look like, or a feeling of it, or you might simply think about it. Let yourself enjoy the experience. You have created what you desired!

Now project yourself five years into the future and imagine that your most important five-year goals have been realized. Again, let yourself enjoy this experience, and express your gratitude. Repeat this exercise one more time with your ten-year goals.

Sharing Your Gifts

The opportunity to share our gifts and thereby make a difference in the world is one of the most profoundly fulfilling experiences we can have in life, and an essential ingredient in creating true prosperity.

Passing on to others what we have received and learned is an important part of completing that process at each level of our healing and growth. We have not fully integrated anything until we have manifested it in our experience in a way that impacts others in some transformational way.

This is not something we have to try to do. It simply happens automatically as we become more aware, do our healing work, and develop and integrate the many aspects of our being. Primarily it happens on an energetic level. The more inner healing we accomplish, the more life force can move through our bodies. This life energy has an impact on everyone we encounter, regardless of our words or actions. The universe literally flows through us to awaken or speed up their transformational process. As we become more conscious, we influence the mass consciousness to shift, which then affects everyone's reality.

Discovering Our Gifts and Talents

As you follow the steps in this workbook you will find yourself naturally expressing and developing the special talents and abilities that you brought with you into this life. When you follow your heart, and are committed to your healing and growth, your simply can't help become more and more of who you are meant to be!

Oftentimes we have difficulty recognizing and appreciating our own talents because they come so naturally to us that they don't seem like any big deal. The things we find ourselves gravitating toward, the things we can't help doing, are important indications of what we are here to do. The things we feel passionate about are clues to our life purpose.

Unless we are blocked in our ability to succeed or receive (in which case we need to do some deep emotional healing work in that area), life always rewards us appropriately for what we give. Through answering what calls to us, we develop our right livelihood. Essentially, the universe pays us to be ourselves as fully as possible!

What are your gifts and talents? Some of them may spring to mind immediately; others may not be so obvious. Some of the exercises on the following pages may help you realize a few additional gifts or talents.

Gifts and Talents Exercise

First, list the gifts and talents that come to your mind immediately below.

You may want to ask a few friends or family members to help you come up with a list of your gifts and talents. Some of their responses may surprise you. Write their responses below:

Make a list below of all the jobs you've ever had. (You may want to include classes or courses of study.) Leave space after each entry to write one or two things that you most enjoyed about the job, followed by one or two things that you least enjoyed about the job:

What activity or activities would you say feed your soul?

Write a list of your accomplishments below. Include those that seem insignificant or "not worth mentioning," such as caring for a sick friend or doing well in a difficult job interview even if you didn't get the job. Those of us who have a particularly unrelenting inner critic or perfectionist tendencies may have a difficult time calling anything an "accomplishment"; all the more reason to list it as an accomplishment below.

Can you think of any beliefs or fears that keep you from sharing the gifts and talents you are aware of?

Asking Your Inner Guidance

Take a few moments to relax your body and mind, then in a deep place within ask yourself the following question: *Are there any specific actions that I need to take to bring my gifts to the world?* Note any responses below.

Expressing Creativity

Discover ways to express your creativity. Everyone is naturally creative, and expressing our creativity is an important part of finding wholeness and fulfillment. In fact, the inability to express our natural creative energy is a root cause of many addictions, as well as much of our spiritual, mental, emotional, and physical pain. The more healing we experience on all levels, the more our creativity begins to emerge.

If you feel your creativity has been blocked, you may need to do some emotional healing, specifically in this area. Get some support to help you discover how and why it got stopped or suppressed, and what is standing in the way of letting it flow.

Getting in touch with and healing your inner child may be a key for unlocking your creativity. Young children are endlessly creative because they have not yet become inhibited. Our creativity often gets dampened or smothered once we begin to develop the inner perfectionist and critic. Our perfectionist tells us how things should be done and sets very high standards for us. Our inner critic points out every time we fall short of perfection. (Being human, this is most of the time!) This can make us unwilling to try new things or express ourselves for fear that we won't do it well enough. We may need to do some conscious healing work with our inner critic and perfectionist, who are actually just trying to protect us from external criticism by trying to shape us to be as perfect as possible. Keeping their best intentions in mind, it can be a good idea to get them to relax a little bit. Then it becomes much easier to contact the naturally spontaneous child within us and encourage him or her to start expressing more in our lives.

To encourage our own creativity we need to lighten up a little bit, have some fun, be adventurous. We need to take some risks to express ourselves in new and different ways. Take small steps first. Try some things that seem fun and creative to you — draw a picture, build something, take a cooking, art, dance, or martial arts class, take up a musical instrument, join an amateur theater group, take up a sport, write a poem or short story, plant a garden. Do it strictly for your own enjoyment, not for anyone else's approval. The purpose of our creativity is our own fulfillment; the goal is not to please other people or win their approval.

Remember that creativity expresses itself in many ways, and each person is unique. You may express your creativity primarily through your work, through raising your children, through a favorite hobby, through remodeling or decorating your home, through the way you dress, or through gardening, cooking, or healing.

The following questions may bring up valuable ideas for expressing your creativity.

What things do you most enjoy doing, or just seem to find yourself doing frequently?

How do you express yourself most easily and naturally?

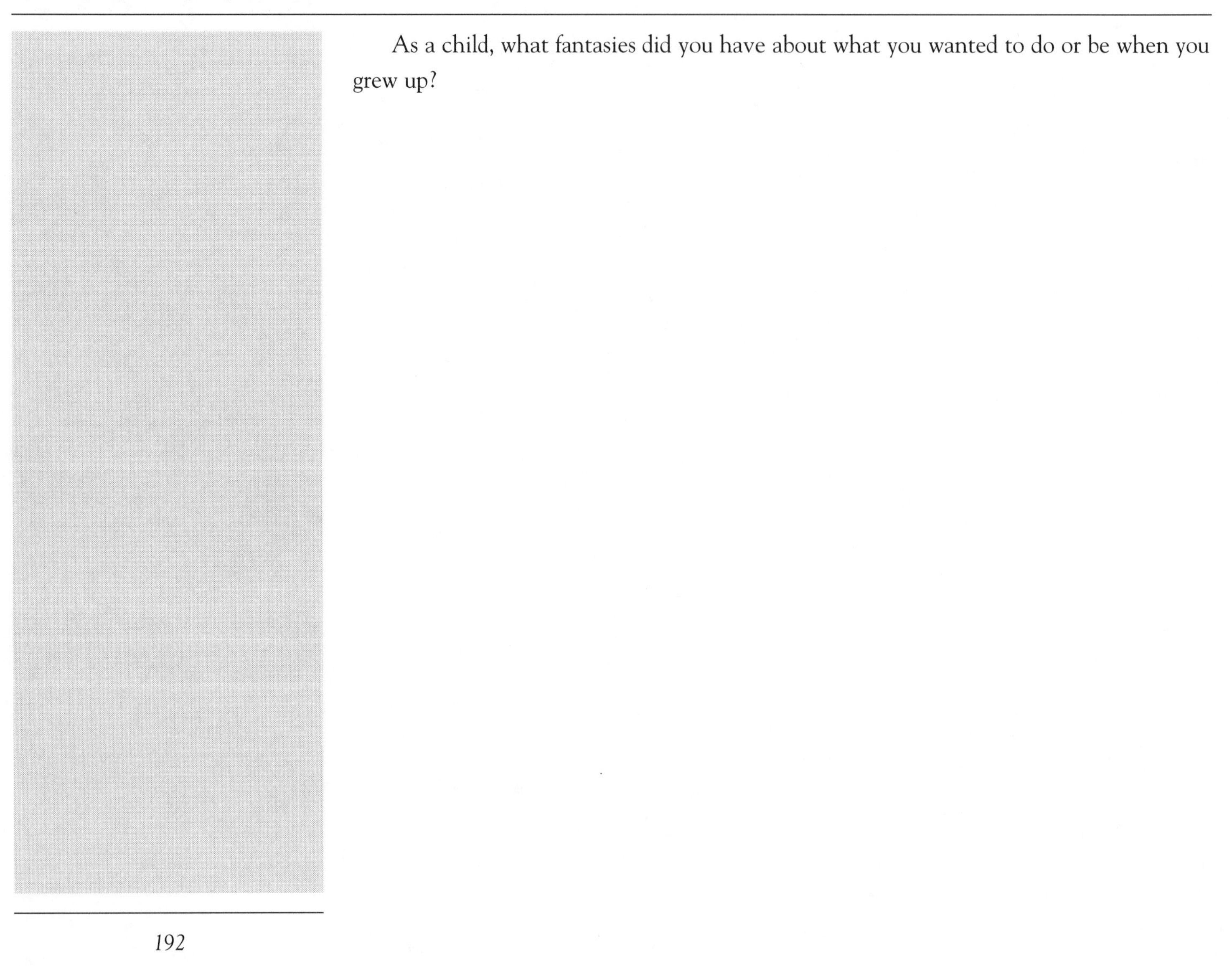

As a child, what fantasies did you have about what you wanted to do or be when you grew up?

Take some time to examine your answers to the previous questions. Can you think of any new ways to begin expressing your creativity? How might some of your childhood fantasies fit into your life today?

Write down any ideas that come to mind below; and if you like, make a commitment to a certain time frame ("this week" or "within the next two weeks") and mark it on your calendar so that the opportunity to express and share your creativity doesn't get lost in the shuffle of a too-busy life. Expressing your creativity is an important part of your prosperity and others' prosperity, too.

Fulfilling Our Higher Purpose

Every one of us comes into this life with lessons to learn and gifts to give. The more we learn and grow, the more we become capable of developing and sharing these natural gifts.

Our higher purpose is what we came here on a soul level to do. We are born with the specific interests, talents, and abilities to fulfill that purpose. In fact, as we come into life we most likely choose the family and environment that will give us the exact combination of support and challenges to overcome obstacles and effectively accomplish our goals. Some of us choose more support in our early life, others choose environments of physical, emotional, mental, and/or spiritual challenge! Regardless of the environment we come from, if we can successfully reap the knowledge that is available in our environment, we are well on our way to recognizing and expressing our higher purpose.

Chances are that our higher purpose is already showing itself in our lives. It is usually there from the very beginning, expressing itself through who we are even as children. Whatever things we do naturally and easily, whatever our innate talents and interests, whatever knowledge and skills we've been led to develop, and whatever people and activities we are drawn to, all these provide us with clues about our higher purpose. We may already be expressing that purpose so naturally and easily that it's just no big deal. If so, we will have a feeling of fulfillment and contentment where that aspect of our lives is concerned.

If you don't feel that you are in touch with your higher purpose, ask your inner guidance to bring you information, awareness, and clarity.

Be patient with yourself. The process of discovering and fulfilling your higher purpose may take years. It cannot be forced or rushed, since it is all part of your unfolding journey.

Allow yourself to be with the questions without demanding answers. When answers do come, they may come in surprising ways and unexpected moments. Keep in mind that doing your consciousness work will automatically bring your higher purpose into focus and clarity over time.

Remember that your higher purpose is not just what you do. It is also who you are — your unique combination of energy, personality, and physical form brings something special into the world. Keep in mind that you have never seen anyone with the same higher purpose as yours, since yours is unique! Your higher purpose has not been invented until you manifest it. Even if you don't feel totally confident in knowing what your higher purpose is, try to put it into words from time to time, until you find a definition that rings perfectly true for you.

When you have finished all the exercises in the workbook that you intend to do, try writing your higher purpose below as accurately and concisely as possible.

My Higher Purpose

Higher Purpose Meditation

Get comfortable, close your eyes, and become aware of your breath. Let your breath take you inside, into a deep, quiet place.

Imagine that you are living your life in alignment with your higher purpose. You are listening to and following your own inner truth, learning and growing from everything you do, and sharing your talents and abilities in a way that is uniquely your own.

Through being fully yourself (including all your human quirks and vulnerabilities) you are touching the lives of others, and making a special contribution to the world.

A Final Thought

Thank you for your courage and commitment to consciousness. I hope that using this workbook has helped you to get to know yourself better and appreciate yourself more than ever. May the work you've done here take you to the next step on your journey into true prosperity.

With love,

Shakti

Calendar

As mentioned in the introduction, this calendar may be used in many different ways:

1) You may want to attach a step to each day of the week to keep you focused on the steps involved in creating true prosperity — Gratitude on Sunday, Awareness on Tuesday, etc.

2) You may want to use the calendar to record your spending and receiving, to record exactly how you are spending your time, or to write in your daily goals and commitments. Anything that helps you take action toward more prosperity or reminds you of the prosperity you are experiencing at this moment can be included.

3) You may want to use the calendar to set up a three-month program — or any length of time that feels right for you — to focus on each of the seven steps presented in the workbook. You can also use it in conjunction with certain exercises in the workbook that require a particular time frame or ask you to keep track of things daily, such as the exercise on tracking your money in the Awareness section.

The calendar is meant to be a tool — so be creative, use it in whatever way works for you, and have fun with it.

September

16	17	18	19
paying debts	bank account	buying for others	buying for myself
24	25	26	27

20
getting my own place
21
vacation
22
car
23
28
29
30
01

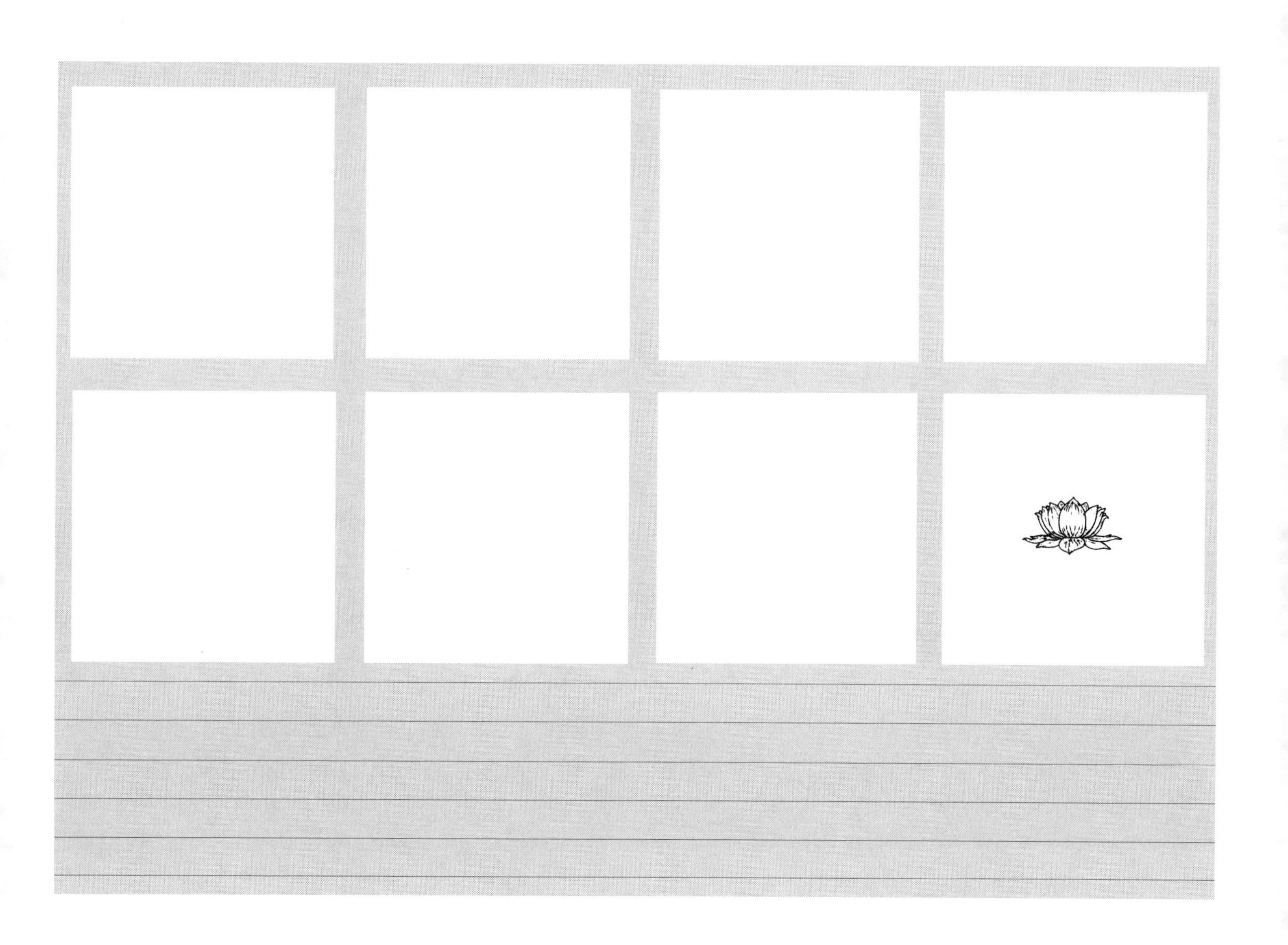

Recommended Resources

Books

Allen, Marc. *Visionary Business: An Entrepreneur's Guide to Success*. New World Library, 1995.

Bryan, Mark and Julia Cameron. *The Money Drunk: 90 Days to Financial Freedom*. Ballantine Books, 1992.

Capacchione, Lucia. *Recovery of Your Inner Child.* Simon & Schuster, 1991.

Gawain, Shakti. *Creating True Prosperity*, Nataraj Publishing/New World Library, 1997.

Gawain, Shakti. *Awakening: A Daily Guide to Conscious Living*. Nataraj Publishing/New World Library, 1991.

Gawain, Shakti. *Creative Visualization*. Nataraj Publishing/New World Library, 1978.

Gawain, Shakti. *Four Levels of Healing: A Guide to Balancing the Spiritual, Mental, Emotional, and Physical Aspects of Life*. Nataraj Publishing/New World Library, 1997.

Gawain, Shakti (with Laurel King). *Living in the Light: A Guide to Personal and Planetary Transformation*. Nataraj Publishing/New World Library, 1986.

Gawain, Shakti. *The Path of Transformation: How Healing Ourselves Can Change the World.* Nataraj Publishing/New World Library, 1993.

Luvaas, Tanha. *Notes from My Inner Child.* Nataraj Publishing/New World Library, 1993.

Orman, Suze. *The Nine Steps to Financial Freedom*. Crown, 1997.

Books

Stone, Hal and Sidra. *Embracing Our Selves: The Voice Dialogue Manual.* Nataraj Publishing/New World Library, 1989.

Stone, Hal and Sidra. *Embracing Each Other: Relationship as Teacher, Healer, and Guide.* Nataraj Publishing/New World Library, 1989.

Stone, Hal and Sidra. *Embracing Your Inner Critic: Turning Self-Criticism into a Creative Asset.* Harper SanFrancisco, 1993.

Stone, Sidra. *The Shadow King: The Invisible Force that Holds Women Back.* Nataraj Publishing/ New World Library, 1997.

Audiotapes

Gawain, Shakti

Creating True Prosperity: Book on Tape. Nataraj Publishing/New World Library, 1997.

Creative Visualization: Book on Tape. Nataraj Publishing/New World Library, 1995.

Creative Visualization Meditations. Nataraj Publishing/ New World Library, 1996.

Audiotapes

The Four Levels of Healing: A Guide to Balancing the Spiritual, Mental, Emotional, and Physical Aspects of Life. Nataraj Publishing/New World Library, 1997.

Living in the Light: Book on Tape. Abridged version. Nataraj Publishing/New World Library, 1993.

Meditations. Nataraj Publishing/New World Library, 1997.

The Path of Transformation: Book on Tape. Abridged version. Nataraj Publishing/New World Library, 1993.

Stone, Hal and Sidra

Meeting Your Selves. Delos, 1990.

The Child Within. Delos, 1990.

Meet Your Inner Critic. Delos, 1990.

Meet the Pusher. Delos, 1990.

The Dance of Selves in Relationship. Delos, 1990.

Understanding Your Relationships. Delos, 1990.

Decoding Your Dreams. Delos, 1990.

These tapes are all available through Drs. Hal and Sidra Stone, P.O. Box 604, Albion, CA 95410-0604 Telephone: (707) 937-2424; E-mail: delos@mcn.org

Videotapes

Gawain, Shakti. *The Path of Transformation.* Videotape of live talk. Hay House, Inc., 1992.

Gawain, Shakti. *Creative Visualization Workshop Video.* Nataraj Publishing/New World Library, 1995.

Gawain, Shakti. *Living in the Light Video.* Zolar Entertainment, 1995.

Workshops

Shakti Gawain gives talks and leads workshops all over the United States and in many other countries. She also conducts retreats, intensives, and training programs. If you would like to be on her mailing list and receive workshop information, contact:

Shakti Gawain, Inc.
P.O. Box 377, Mill Valley, CA 94942
Telephone: (415) 388-7140
Fax: (415) 388-7196
E-mail: sg@nataraj.com
www.shaktigawain.com

Workshops

For individuals and couples wishing to come for personal retreats, Shakti and her husband, Jim Burns, rent rooms and a guest cottage at their beautiful estate on the Hawaiian island of Kaua'i. Shakti also conducts week-long intensives on Kaua'i. For information or to make a reservation, contact:

Kai Mana
P.O. Box 612, Kilauea, HI 96754
Telephone: (808) 828-1280 or (800) 837-1782
Fax: (808) 828-6670
www.kai-mana.com

For information about Drs. Hal and Sidra Stone's workshops and trainings, contact:

Delos
P.O. Box 604, Albion, CA 95410
Telephone: (707) 937-2424
E-mail: delos@mcn.org

Nataraj Publishing, a division of New World Library, is dedicated to publishing books and cassettes that inspire and challenge us to improve the quality of our lives and our world.

Our books and tapes are available in bookstores everywhere. For a catalog of our complete library of fine books and cassettes contact:

NATARAJ PUBLISHING/NEW WORLD LIBRARY
14 PAMARON WAY
NOVATO, CA 94949
TEL: (415) 884-2100
FAX: (415) 884-2199
OR CALL TOLL-FREE: (800) 972-6657
CATALOG REQUESTS: EXT. 50
ORDERING: EXT. 52
E-MAIL: ESCORT@NWLIB.COM
HTTP://WWW.NWLIB.COM